# Beyond Armageddon
*Creating the New Age of Aquarius*

© Worldwide Copyright 2003 Arberton International Ltd.. All rights reserved.

First Published 2003 by Arberton International Ltd.

Arberton International Ltd asserts the right to be identified as the official representative of the author in accordance with the Copyright, Designs, and Patents Act of 1998

Website: www.arberton.com

No part of this publication may be reproduced, stored in or introduced into a retrieval system, or transmitted, in any form, or by any means (electronic, mechanical, photocopying, recording or otherwise) without the prior written permission of the publisher. Any person who does any unauthorized act in relation to this publication may be liable to criminal prosecution and civil claims for damages.

Printed in Victoria, Canada

```
National Library of Canada Cataloguing in Publication Data

The Amanuensis
        Beyond Armageddon : creating the New Age of Aquarius / The
Amanuensis.
Includes bibliographical references and index.
ISBN 1-4120-0373-3
       I. Title.
BS649.A68T48 2003            001.9              C2003-902817-8
```

# TRAFFORD

Suite 6E, 2333 Government St., Victoria, B.C. V8T 4P4, CANADA
Phone      250-383-6864       Toll-free    1-888-232-4444 (Canada & US)
Fax        250-383-6804       E-mail       sales@trafford.com
Web site   www.trafford.com   TRAFFORD PUBLISHING IS A DIVISION OF TRAFFORD HOLDINGS LTD.
Trafford Catalogue #03-0741   www.trafford.com/robots/03-0741.html

10     9     8     7     6     5     4     3

# Beyond Armageddon
*Creating the New Age of Aquarius*

by
The Amanuensis

Arberton International Ltd.
www.arberton.com

# Dedication

This book is dedicated to the Masters of Wisdom of the Great Brotherhood of Light.

# Contents

| | |
|---|---|
| Preface | 5 |
| Chapter 1—Some Fundamentals | 9 |
| Chapter 2—The Great Brotherhood of Light | 18 |
| Chapter 3—The Dark Forces Today | 30 |
| Chapter 4—Control of the Nation-State | 52 |
| Chapter 5—Pillaging of the Private Sector | 74 |
| Chapter 6—Masters of War | 97 |
| Chapter 7—The Armageddon | 107 |
| Chapter 8—The Reconstruction | 127 |
| Postscript | 145 |

# Preface

Many fear the dreaded Armageddon is now upon us. Some say the end of the world is nigh. We agree that the Armageddon is indeed upon us, but we can assure you that the end of the world is not even close at hand. Instead, the Piscean Age that has been with us for over two thousand years is drawing to a close and a new one, the Aquarian Age, is being born. As we transit from one age to another, there is always turmoil.

How do we know this? We base our opinion on the ancient wisdom of the Masters of the Great Brotherhood of Light. They have assured us that the Armageddon is indeed upon us. Its function is not to annihilate the world, but rather, to flush out the evildoers. When it is over, the good and innocent will remain to rebuild the earth into the promised Age of Aquarius.

It is thus, the purpose of this book to inform the world that doom does not await mankind on the other side of the present world conflict. Instead, mankind can look forward to a marvelous journey toward enlightenment, throwing off the Adamic chains and continuing on the ascent to enlightenment.

The Masters of Wisdom are ever-present in spirit,

well within the purview of earth but in another dimension. At times, they materialize physically to communicate with their initiates or disciples. Clairvoyant persons communicate regularly with them as they have done throughout time. Clairvoyant prophets and scribes wrote many great spiritual works of the past and present such as the Bible, Kabala, and Koran. But the communication did not stop there.

In this book, we will introduce you to the Great Brotherhood of Light and the Masters who, unbeknownst to most, communicate and influence matters on earth telepathically, materializing only in key instances. The Brotherhood continued, as they have done for millennia, to influence the thinking of writers, musicians, scientists, philosophers, politicians, bankers, and others, from all walks of life. Their mission through the ages has been to evolve and expand man's intellect arriving at this current point in time: where mankind now actively seeks to communicate with the Brotherhood. It is through this written material, They hope to communicate their views to more open-minded people resident on earth today.

I only recently came to know about the Great Brotherhood of Light. Up to that momentous event, I received a normal education in the universities of America and Europe learning earthly logic and scientific methods of inquiry. I later applied this knowledge to an international career in diplomacy, foreign assistance, and business. Yet, none of this earthly training and experience could have prepared me for this new adventure in telepathic communication with the Brothers of the Great Brotherhood of Light. This rather late psychic development had its purpose, for it has given me the time to learn more about the concrete world and interpret in more detail what the Masters of Wisdom want us to know about our world today.

The final battle between light and darkness, the Armageddon, is now upon us. Most of us are led to believe that the whole world will blow up in flames, but the Armageddon is subtler than that. Yes, wars will also abound for the next decade, but for centuries the forces of darkness have been building a nexus of enslavement around mankind that has engulfed it in materialism and human conflict. This nexus also has to be dismantled, for it brings to every level of society, family disorders, upheavals in time-tried relationships, and just plain insanity. And to aggravate matters even further, a deep economic depression upon humanity will also bring about this dismantlement.

All this turmoil is for a good purpose. By putting the insanity and conflict of the Armageddon in its proper perspective and maintaining a steady view of what is on the other side of this decade of great turmoil, we can see a period of reconstruction that will prepare a truly wonderful Golden Age for mankind. The Brotherhood is confident that when mankind realizes the chains that have been built around it, humanity will be glad that the Armageddon is upon us. We want to assure you that there is indeed a very bright light at the end of this tunnel.

We present our ideas to you as merely food –for-thought. We do not seek to argue, convince, or coddle the reader into accepting them. We merely wish to raise certain questions and present you with a different, yet very plausible way, of looking at events in the world. Our views are often in direct contradiction to what is commonly presented in the world's media and may be difficult to fathom. We will raise questions concerning terrorism, war, the national debt, taxation, bureaucracy, and the stock market decline in the context of earth's evolution. In doing so, we hope to explain the reason for the Armageddon and how it will lead to a Golden Age, the likes of which the earth has never seen. So hang on. We're in for a rough ride, but the glory and light at the end of the tunnel make it all worth it.


The Amanuensis
July, 2003

# CHAPTER 1
## Some Fundamentals

### Introduction

Before we delve into the subject of the Armageddon, let us review a few esoteric precepts concerning the present situation on earth. You need not agree with or believe in these precepts: you need only understand our underlying assumptions about the universe and man, for they determine our outlook and interpretation of current events.

### Assumptions

#### Earth's Evolution

Each and every individual is a spark of energy emanating from the great cosmic energy force we call God, the Creator. In fact, everything—even a planetary body in the universe—is linked to God by its own spark of energy. You, for example, are a spark of energy "wearing" or wrapped by a human body. The planet earth is a larger spark of energy directly emanating from God, while the whole solar system, one of many comprising a sun and its planets, is also a huge spark of energy emanating from the same Source. Whatever the size of the spark, it is the *soul* of whatever it inhabits; the spark of energy that runs through your body and gives it life is your soul or Higher Self that is directly connected to the Creator, no matter what body you might be wearing at any point in time.

When the Creator breathes out, all the sparks of energy scatter throughout space, some traveling millions of years to take their positions in the universe according to the Divine Plan. This is the great creation in all its multitudinous forms. When the Creator inhales, all the sparks of energy return back to their Creator. Each cycle of "out breath" and "in breath" of the Creator takes millions and millions of earth years and is beyond human calculation.

When we say, "This being is more highly evolved" or "This planet is higher on the evolutionary ladder," we are generally referring to the inhalation phase of creation, e.g., the trip back to the Source. The farther the spark is located from the Source, the lower it will be on the evolutionary scale, so conversely, the closer a spark is to the Source, the higher its evolution. When the Creator inhales, it draws back its multitudinous sparks, and the closer these sparks get to the Source, the purer their form must become to eventually merge back into the Source, the Creator.

The spark that is Earth reached its destination in space several hundred thousand years ago, and since then, has been struggling to get back on track for its journey back to the Creator. Today, we find ourselves in the inhalation part of the cosmic cycle: both earth and its inhabitants have now started the million year-plus journey back to the Creator. The period emerging as the Age of

Aquarius will put us firmly back on the Path of return or inhalation. As we evolve back to the Source, the material forms that we recognize as the planet earth, and its inhabitants, will gradually take on more and more ephemeral forms. We explain further along in this material how certain individual souls at their own choosing, can elect to evolve back at a faster pace than the rest of humanity, and like scouts ahead of the pack, they guide us along the path.

**Spirit and Matter**

Many of the traditional religions have tried to make a distinction between these two concepts creating of them polar opposites. In reality, we consider them one and the same. Take for example an individual spark or soul that the Creator sends out into space. The farther the spark goes out, the slower its velocity. As the spark gets farther and farther away, the energy vibrations get slower and slower and manifest as what we call matter. What we thus observe as material objects, including our human bodies, is that same spark of energy vibrating at a slower rate. This is why we consider spirit and matter as one and the same energy only vibrating at different rates.

As we evolve back to the Source, our souls take on a higher vibratory rate, which is why our bodies will become "less material." As we will see below, the souls of Masters of the Great Brotherhood of Light have advanced to the point where they can manifest their material bodies at will by controlling the vibrations of their bodies, yet they can quickly restore their high energy vibrations and disappear from our eyesight.

### Reincarnation

The trip of a million years back to the Creator obviously cannot be achieved within one puny lifetime, neither can all the lessons be learned within that short lifetime to achieve the high level of the Masters of Wisdom. It is therefore most logical to conclude that our souls must wear thousands of bodies over a vast period of time to evolve back to the Creator in the purest form possible. Here on earth, the same soul reincarnates countless times until the lessons on earth have been "passed" and the soul no longer sees any need to continue the reincarnations. So, all of us have been rulers, doctors, prelates, lawyers, merchants, and thieves in both male and female bodies.

A survey of mankind today shows countless levels of incarnations in progress. Some are very old souls who will probably pass into more ephemeral forms of adepts; they are anxious to make a leap into the more evolved forms. Others are very young souls just beginning their journey of a million years. However, the vast majority of mankind is just muddling along, making a little progress here and there, but mostly struggling under the yoke of forces that have sought to oppress them and stymie their progress.

## Cosmic Origins of the Great Brotherhood of Light

The long trip back to the Creator implies a particular struggle, a struggle borne of the inertia in matter, or slow vibratory energy. Many millennia ago, more evolved beings from other planets that have already passed through earth's present stage of evolution, were sent to earth to help guide earth and its inhabitants. These advanced ones helped prepare earth for its return trip by training particularly bright earthly humans to take over their work as earth's cosmic guides. They recruited disciples from among earth's population whose souls had passed through countless earth bound incarnations in order to learn earth's lessons, its trials, and tribulations.

These disciples evolved at a faster pace than the rest of humanity. They finally attained to more ephemeral bodies when they ascended into the higher dimensions of evolution and became Masters. Some of these Masters have reached such a high degree of perfection that they visit other more advanced planets, such as earth's sister planet Venus, and beyond. Some of these Masters choose to remain with earth instead of moving onto higher evolutions in order to help mankind as a whole evolve further.

Over many millennia, these highly evolved beings formed a core known as the Great Brotherhood of Light whose purpose was and is to guide earth's inhabitants on its evolutionary path back to the Creator. These Masters work under and coordinate their activities with those great cosmic beings who guide the evolution of earth itself. Having evolved at a faster pace, the Great Brotherhood of Light is in a sense the vanguard of the human race—the role models of what we ourselves will be like millennia from now.

## Cosmic Origins of The Dark Forces

One of the peculiar characteristics of earth is that it lies in the free-will zone of the universe, and as such, can attract beings from other planets that have failed or chosen not to evolve with their own populations. In other words, throwbacks or dropouts from other planetary evolutions can choose to live on earth to work out further their salvation. By the cosmic Law of Attraction those dropouts from other evolutions tend to be those of the same degree of evolution as we are on earth. Many of these dropouts date back to the days of Atlantis that ancient but advanced civilization that once covered a major part of the earth's surface. Atlantis destroyed itself at the very stage of evolution we find ourselves today. These Atlantean dropouts have been waiting in the wings, so to speak, on the astral plane, until the time they can rejoin earth. In other words, Atlantis had reached the point in a previous astrological cycle where its Piscean Age was transiting into the Aquarian Age, just as we are now, and it was at that point that they destroyed themselves. Those benighted ones, who were in part responsible for its demise, have now found a home in our present civilization.

Some dropouts rejoined earth only to rediscover the Path of Light and righteousness, and during that time they were redeemed. However, many of them held stubbornly to their Atlantean ways and now, form the core of what we call The Dark Forces on earth. These benighted ones expelled their highly evolved spiritual leadership on Atlantis and took over the power structure. They experimented with martial force and money to bring vast segments of the Atlantean population under their subjugation. In the end, their methods caused the ultimate collapse of Atlantis.

Over the past few centuries, these throwbacks of Atlantis and other planetary evolutions have banded together in what we call The Dark Mixing with the good and innocent souls that were originally destined for earth, they have created a heterogeneous mix of souls quite unlike any other planet in this solar system. Their presence on earth accounts for all the strife and conflict we have been experiencing over the ages as they thwart mankind's attempts to stay on the Divine evolutionary path. Throughout the tumultuous Twentieth Century, we witnessed the likes of Adolph Hitler, Josef Stalin, and the generals of the Emperor Hirohito slaughter masses of humans in their bid to subjugate the populations of earth. Today, their likes exist in greater numbers. Some engage in activities as cold blooded and ruthless as in previous generations. Others wear sheep's clothing, while using much more subtle tactics, to prey on the weaknesses of humanity and gradually enslave it.

## Project of the Master Sanctus Germanus

As earth's Piscean cycle comes to an end, the Great Brotherhood of Light has determined to cast The Dark Forces off the earth before it can enter the New Age, the Age of Aquarius, for as long as they remain on earth, mankind will be diverted from its true evolution. Many advanced souls, past luminaries in human history, have chosen to reincarnate to join the battle on the side of mankind.

Over the past few decades, the battle lines of a final conflict have been drawn and the forces of the Great Brotherhood of Light under the guidance and direction of the Great and Holy Master Sanctus Germanus are now poised to fight the final battle. The final battle between the light and darkness is what is commonly known symbolically as the Armageddon. The outcome of that battle has already been determined, for this time the light forces shall prevail and the benighted souls will be banished from the earth plane forever.

So this is why the Armageddon, rather than being the end of the world, is actually the purging of these evil influences from earth. So we believe the playing out of the Armageddon will set the stage for a new Golden Age where earth regains its momentum up the evolutionary ladder and back to the Creator.

## Individual Evolution

The Masters of the Great Brotherhood of Light whose ranks include highly evolved beings who "came up from the ranks," so to speak, of earth's tortuous school, serve as examples of what can be accomplished by the exercise of free will. Their example serves to illustrate a major point in the evolutionary scheme–that each individual soul can decide to accelerate its evolution. The individual soul need not be held back by the pace of things on earth, or because of the masses of mankind. Those adepts or luminaries who live among us are souls who have broken rank, so to speak, and chosen to follow the Path of evolution at an accelerated pace. How is this possible?

Of these billions of souls sent to earth, there are no two alike and therefore no two human beings are alike. Even identical twins house two different souls, which accounts for the difference in their personalities. Some souls evolve faster than others. Some will have had more incarnations than others and have spent more time on earth than others.

These obvious differences account for why some are more spiritually evolved than others but it is the nature of free will in earth's zone that permits the soul to make its own decision concerning its own evolution back to the Creator. In other words, some souls choose a fast track while others take their time.

Some souls become so imbibed with earth's material pleasures and pains that they choose not to follow the path of evolution. As The Dark Forces have taken over the mass media and propagated their short-term views on life, many innocent and weak-minded have been drawn into their ranks. They become ready victims and tools of The Dark Forces primarily in the form of flunkies, fall guys, or petty criminals, whose activities are designed "to take the heat," and distract the public's attention, while the greater more heinous crimes against humanity are being committed. This of course is a temporary condition for all must eventually follow the Path; even if it takes millennia to accomplish.

### The "I AM" Dispensation

Those who consciously take the decision to stand on the side of light must come to the realization of the divine presence, the "I AM," or the soul that resides within them. When they come to realize that the "I AM" presence or soul is the spark of energy linking them directly with God, the Creator, they learn to call upon it as something to be adored, to be acknowledged, and to be grateful for. They realize that this magic presence of the soul is the gift of all gifts, the God-Self of the individual. This is the Self that one must repair to constantly and daily, to give all gratitude to the great "I AM" presence and derive all good from IT. When we commune with IT, often through meditation, we can ask IT to flood our world with all its perfection, and in doing so, we systematically set loose the force of light that sweeps away human foolishness, blindness, stupidity, and those evils that surround our lives. This simple realization is the David that slays the Goliath in the battle of the Armageddon that is before us.

# CHAPTER 2

## The Great Brotherhood of Light

We have mentioned The Great Brotherhood of Light briefly in the previous chapter. This Brotherhood of highly evolved and perfected beings came to be known fairly recently to western civilization at the end of the Nineteenth Century. Helena P. Blavatsky and Henry Steel Olcott, both representative spirits of the Great Brotherhood of Light, founded the Theosophical Society in 1875 and revealed in their writings the existence this body of highly evolved beings, which played a major role in the evolution of earth's affairs. Known among the mystics in the early part of the Piscean Age, most Christians knew nothing of such a Brotherhood, except in underground mystery schools such as the Masonic and Rosicrucian movements. On the other side of the world however, the peoples of India and the Far East including China and Japan had for centuries revered and worshipped the many adepts of the Brotherhood.

Every religion, every god or goddess, every major historical event, every artistic wave, every political, or social movement has come to pass under the influence of

# Great Brotherhood of Light

the Brotherhood. The Prophet Mohammed, the Master Jesus, the Master Gautama Buddha, and the Master Confucius were all incarnations of highly evolved beings of the Brotherhood When the Theosophical Movement revealed the existence of the Brotherhood, it created quite an uproar in the west. Victorian intellectuals wanted solid, scientific proof of their existence. Christians condemned Theosophy as heresy and the mixing of pagan philosophies utter blasphemy. Even the Spiritualists considered all this talk of Masters to be verging on insanity.

Yet, the Theosophical Movement pursued its path under the guidance of the Great and Holy Masters Kuthumi and El Morya. Its cofounder, Col. Henry Steel Olcott, described the Great Brotherhood of Light as follows:

> . . . (T)here is and ever was but one altruistic alliance, or fraternity, of these Elder Brothers of humanity, the world over; but it is divided into sections according to the needs of the human race in its successive stages of evolution. In one age the focal center of this world-helping force will be in one place, in another elsewhere. Unseen, and suspected as the vivifying spiritual currents of the Akash, yet as indispensable for the spiritual welfare of mankind, their combined divine energy is maintained from age to age and forever refreshes the pilgrim of earth, who struggles on towards the divine reality. The sceptic denies the existence of these Adepts because he has not seen or talked with them, nor read the history of their visible intermeddling in national events. But their being

has been known to thousands of self-illuminate mystics and philanthropists in succeeding generations, whose purified souls have lifted them up out of the muck of physical into the brightness of spiritual consciousness; and at many epochs they have come into personal relations with the persons who are devoting or inclined to devote themselves to altruistic labor for bringing about the brotherhood of mankind. Olcott, Henry Steel, *Old Diary Leaves*, volume 1.

The point made here is that the activities of the Great Brotherhood of Light, although unseen to the normal human senses, permeate every avenue of life. Nothing that man has invented has been able to blunt or quiet the influence of the Great Brotherhood of Light throughout what we might call modern civilization. How does the Great Brotherhood of Light operate?

The Great Brotherhood of Light consists of highly evolved souls, who exist in another dimension within earth's atmosphere. It could be said that their headquarters is located on the etheric plane in a city called Shamballa in the Himalayan mountain range. However, since communication between Brotherhood members is instantaneous, the Masters of the Brotherhood are found all over the world, where they are needed. There are regional headquarters of the Brotherhood on every continent, all existing on the etheric plane beyond the limited five senses of the common man.

The Masters of the Brotherhood represent the human race of the future and therefore are able to lead us in the right direction as we evolve according to the Divine Plan. When we speak of the future, we mean tens of thousands of years hence. The Brotherhood comprises vast numbers of advanced and perfected beings, who have consciously chosen to remain within earth's atmosphere, to help the rest of humanity evolve, instead of moving onto a more advanced planetary body. Many of them are of such an advanced evolution that they can come and go at will between planetary bodies. A much frequented planet is Venus, the sister planet of earth.

The Masters no longer need to wear the dense physical bodies we carry but exist in lighter, more ethereal forms of matter which we call spirit. They can, however, materialize temporarily to the point where the common man can perceive them. They can be in several places at the same time, and their extraordinary intelligence and perceptions make it possible for them to discern our thoughts and instantaneously respond to them.

The Masters today communicate with us through telepathy—thought transference from spirit to the human brain. Their messages of truth touch our individual souls and are then stepped down and filtered through our subconscious minds, then to our conscious minds, and finally to the brain. Much of this transmission is carried out while we are in a state of sleep and when the physical body does not pose too much a resistance to receiving telepathic messages. During our waking hours, those of good heart and motives receive these thoughts clairvoyantly oft times not realizing from where they come.

Clairvoyants who can hear or see the Masters are called mediums. Many initiates and disciples incarnated on earth communicate with their Masters in this manner. At times, the Masters will address congregations of people through mediums. Other times, they will materialize temporarily to communicate something important to a particular person, then leave. Sometimes, they may even materialize as an adept to instruct a group of disciples over a period of time, then evaporate. Or they may speak to a person in his dreams and impress his conscious mind with certain ideas.

The Masters are known to leave certain apports as proof of their presence. These materialized objects—gems, jewelry, medals and the like—were used by Mme. Blavatsky to convince a hardened, skeptical and intellectual Victorian mindset during her time. Today, the Masters leave these phenomena with their initiates and disciples as evidence of their ever-presence and guidance.

Certain Masters concentrate on certain fields of endeavor. For example, the Master in charge of the labor movement on earth will impress upon the labor leaders certain directions the movement should take. The leaders are not necessarily aware of the source of ideas, yet advocate them as their own. The Master Sanctus Germanus is known to have impressed upon the founders of the American Republic the contents of the Declaration of Independence and the U.S. Another Master may impress his thinking about a certain medical research project to solve an epidemic, while another may inspire a composer, without his knowledge, to write an extraordinary symphony. So it is that the Masters of the Brotherhood have changed the course of human history and raised its level of evolution with radical ideas over the centuries.

According to the Cosmic Law of Free Will, the Masters can only impress and suggest ideas to mankind. They cannot impose. So the recipient is free to reject, modify, or follow them.

## Hierarchy, A Fact of Life, A Cosmic Reality

Cosmic law organizes this enormous pool of differing soul evolution into a great cosmic hierarchical structure stretching from the infinite Creator all the way down to the basic atom. This structure is reflected in our own human society. Every group or organization is organized in a hierarchical manner. Everyone has someone above him and below him. Even in the smallest group, there is a leader. It is noteworthy to observe that even those advocates of human equality, e.g., democracy, socialism, and communism have all ended up creating some of history's largest hierarchies.

A proper, spiritual hierarchical structure does not dominate. It is by nature a hierarchy of love, one that promotes upward mobility. Each soul occupies a certain level of the hierarchy according to its level of spiritual evolution. Those on the upper levels guide and help it to advance upward. As it advances in spiritual growth, it moves up the ladder of evolution.

The Cosmic Law of Hierarchy is a fact of life, a cosmic reality in the Universe. Hierarchy's main function is to preserve and protect the divine order and wisdom. The individual can take comfort that there is always someone superior to him whose greater knowledge can help and protect him, and someone below him, whom he can in turn teach and protect.

Here on the earth plane, hierarchy translates into a condition in nature where there is always a leader, a ruler, or one of superior position. The lower kingdoms—mineral, vegetable, and animal—are also organized in some sort of hierarchy. And within each kingdom is also a complex hierarchy of sub-kingdoms. In the human kingdom, each family, society, institution, and governmental structure reflects this universal hierarchical structure.

Any individual who claims he is an independent entity outside hierarchy is deluding himself, for it is usually one who has been subjected to domination within a hierarchy who fears and often rebels against it. And yet, they unfortunately end up often being told what to do by everyone.

## The Inner Governing Structure of the World

The world today is divided into nation-states within which is a hierarchical governmental structure. On the international level, there is a network of international organizations such as the United Nations and regional organizations consisting of nation-states. Yet, beyond this earthly political structure exists a blanket hierarchy, covering the whole of earth's political hierarchical structures, a divine chain of command or divine governing hierarchy. This is the Inner Government or power structure of the Great Brotherhood of Light

Earth's inner spiritual government is in charge of implementing the Great Divine Plan that was drawn up for earth millions of years ago. Each of the billions of souls involved with life on earth is part of this Plan and each is guided to carry out his or her particular task and role.

A council comprising three offices— the World Teacher, the Executive (Mahachohan) and Facilitator (Divine Will)—heads the current inner spiritual government. The Lord Maitreya headed the Office of the World Teacher during the Piscean Age. It was He who overshadowed the Master Jesus during his last three exceptional years as the Messiah on earth. Now, the Great and Holy Master Kuthumi has assumed this office and will set forth the cosmic principles that will govern the New Age throughout the Aquarian Dispensation. He has the vast task of educating all of mankind of these principles.

The Office of the Executive or Mahachohan is held by the Great and Holy Master Sanctus Germanus, who coordinates multitudinous activities to prepare the world for the return of World Teacher. He leads the battle of the Light Forces against those of darkness during the Armageddon. This office requires massive coordination of the various Masters and their respective groups and initiates, all working to fulfill their respective tasks according to the Divine Plan.

Finally, the third office of this triumvirate body is the Facilitator, occupied by the Great and Holy Master Morya. He represents the Divine Will, the impetus and power that implement policies and educational programs of the two other offices of the World Teacher and the Executive. Representing the Divine Will, the Master Morya finds the most effective path; the path of least resistance to go from A to B; and the power to implement and realize a policy in the most efficient, energy-saving way.

Working with these three principal Masters are the Great and Holy Masters Djwal Khul and JMH (one of many aliases). The Master Djwal Khul assists in the liaison work between the Office of the World Teacher and those initiates and disciples on earth. The Master JMH assists the Office of the Executive (Mahachohan) in areas of international politics, economics, and finance and intelligence. All five Masters supervise ashrams with thousands of workers in various committees to carry out the final transition from the Piscean to the Aquarian Age, in line with the Divine Plan.

For example, under the Master Kuthumi, there is a committee made up of ex-prelates of the major world religions who are editing all the scriptures (the Bible, Koran, Kabala, Gita Bhaghavad, etc.) so that they conform to the needs of the coming Aquarian Age. Another committee under the Master JMH's supervision monitors the financial machinations of the financiers behind The Dark Forces. Lady Masters of the Brotherhood prepare women for their advanced role in peacemaking as the Feminine Ray descends upon the events of the Armageddon. Other Masters work among those in the performing and creative arts, religion, culture, literature, sciences, academia, and the like, all with the aim of lifting man's thinking and culture.

The nature and breadth of the activities of the Inner Government reach every sector of life on earth. Some are aware of their intervention but the vast majority of mankind remains completely ignorant of their influence.

## Government by the Divine Plan

The Divine Plan for earth has been in existence since time immemorial and is unfathomable to the limited human mind. However, from time to time, avatars and messengers appear on earth to reveal bits and pieces of the Plan. At this particular juncture of the Plan, the triumvirate body is in full swing preparing mankind for the eventual approach of the World Teacher. Traditional religions have often spoken of the second coming of their principal teachers. But this time, there will be one Teacher. We do not know what form the World Teacher will take, but it is possible that the World Teacher will not take a human form as in the past but rather, represent a vast body of teachings aimed at all levels of mankind and disseminated through the mass media.

Before mankind can receive these teachings, earth must perform a massive housecleaning, for without this purification the teachings of the World Teacher will go unheard or again fall into the morass of conflicting religions as in the past. This is the reason for the so-called Armageddon, which will purge and sift out all the evil elements on earth, throughout the vast hierarchy from the lowest to the highest and vice versa. Only after this great purgation will humanity be ready for the revolutionary teachings of the World Teacher.

## Masters and Adepts on the Earth Plane

Adepts of the Brotherhood, appearing in the physical body, also walk among mankind quietly and discreetly. Their physical and spiritual presence has been more marked during these recent decades for reasons we will cover in the next chapter. Around these adepts are their initiates, disciples, and workers who are spread throughout the earth. More pressing today, given the events of the Armageddon, these adepts walk among us to prepare mankind for the transition into the Aquarian Age.

Some Masters of the Great Brotherhood of Light, who materialize among us, are already known to the occult world. The Great and Holy Master Sanctus Germanus usually takes on the form of his most famous incarnation as the Comte de St. Germain, although this does not stop him from masquerading as any personality he chooses. The Master JMH is known to "crash" important financial convocations such as the meetings of the world's finance ministers, religious leaders, trade and economic bodies, and the more sinister meetings of The Dark Forces. The point here is that they will masquerade in whatever form that will accomplish the task at hand.

Other Masters of the Brotherhood prefer to impress their advice through telepathy, transferring their thoughts and ideas to those clairvoyant minds willing and developed enough to accept them. There are still other Masters who untiringly impress progressive and innovative ideas upon statesmen, artists, scientists, writers, clergy, and other open minds individuals, often without their knowledge. This constant flow of revelation accounts for the scientific breakthroughs, sublime artistic achievements, and turn of international events for the better we experience on earth.

Disciples of the Masters who are in spirit and who are working diligently on the Divine Plan are known to take over the bodies of those already incarnated. These are called "walk-ins." Often by previous agreement, a soul will incarnate and take the body to a certain stage in life at which time a new and often higher soul will "walk in" and take over the body while the previous soul consents to exit. The new occupier of the body will retain all memory and characteristics of the body, but often their friends will note subtle changes. Sometimes, a soul might be very depressed and want to leave the world, at which time, a walk-in may be proposed and accepted. Usually, walk-ins result in a step up in evolution.

The Inner Government of the Brotherhood even stretches its influence below the human plane. Working with *devas* or fairy-like creatures, they influence the lower animals, plants, and mineral kingdoms. The physical phenomena and apports produced by great occult luminaries such as Helena P. Blavatsky and the mysterious adept, JMH, demonstrate the kind of benevolent control the Brotherhood maintains on these kingdoms.

Some may ask, "Why don't the Masters just take

over the whole world and straighten it out once and for all?" The answer to this is quite simple. The Masters must abide by the Cosmic Law of freewill that is particular to mankind. If the Masters were to do everything, how would the pupil learn?

# CHAPTER 3
## The Dark Forces Today
"By their fruits, ye shall know them."

Terrorist attacks and spot conflicts around the world, including the ongoing Israeli-Arab war, the Indo-Pakistani conflicts, the Tamil-Singhalese guerilla war on Sri Lanka, the war in Afghanistan against the so-called Al Qaeda terrorists, the Muslim uprisings in the Philippines, the tensions in the Taiwan straits between China and Taiwan, and the host of other ethnic and genocidal wars taking place in the Balkans and central Africa are all designed to keep the world in a state of perpetual division and conflict. As soon as one conflict is resolved, others pop up in a never-ending state of warfare.

The attack on the New York World Trade Center on September 11 shocked the world as it was designed to. But the true story of this attack and other conflicts in the world today are not what the popular media portrays. In essence, what is manifesting on earth is the reflection of the battle being waged on the astral plane between the Great Brotherhood of Light and The Dark Forces that inhabit the earth. The mighty spear has already been lanced through the heart of the great dragon of evil, spelling the end to the heyday of The Dark Forces on earth. As the dragon succumbs, its tail flails in agony, and with each whiplash of the tail, we feel the wave of turmoil sweep through the earth plane. On earth, The Dark Forces are desperately trying to make a final grab for all the power they will need to suppress the mass of humanity and place themselves on top of the world . . . so they think. The forces of light have already determined the outcome of this battle on earth, the Armageddon, the final battle between good and evil, and they are doomed.

In this chapter we wish to share our observations of how The Dark Forces operate today. The better-informed humanity is, the better prepared it is to mentally resist any more of their evil works. Be assured that man's mental resistance has incalculable power to speed up the inevitable demise of The Dark Forces.

We must emphasize to you, the reader, that the esoteric facts put forth here should be considered food-for-thought. Some of you may be shocked or outraged at what we say, but whatever human reaction our words provoke, our intention is simply to inform and to educate, with the hope that all things shall be understood in due time. We are not here to coddle, neither are we here to flatter, nor to frighten much less. Nor are we here to bring some kind of protection salve against some evil force, because in reality we do not believe in evil to begin with. The closest thing we can call evil is *ignorance*. For it is only when the soul is profoundly ignorant that it tends to do those things that people call evil.

Until most recently, most esoteric literature has treated information on The Dark Forces quite gingerly, for it was always in the heart of the Brotherhood that these benighted ones, also creations of God, would one day choose the path of light. Some have been transformed, but unfortunately many more have not and continue to follow a dark path that wrecks havoc on earth.

## Why the Dark Brethren Incarnate on Earth

We mentioned in the previous chapter that The Dark Forces consist of dropouts from more advanced evolutions. You may ask why the dark brethren are permitted to incarnate on earth to carry out their dastardly deeds. Earth is in the free will zone of the universe and any soul or soul-shell can decide to incarnate on earth. In our particular level of evolution, we learn by trial and error. That is the way of things at the Planetary School Board, so to speak. We all come into the flesh as individuals, learning as individuals, and en masse as part of our culture and society. We must choose between the high and low, the good and bad, the right and wrong. This way only shall we truly discover truth. The presence of The Dark Forces on earth provides a polarity, and a choice given all incarnates between good and evil.

When a choice is kept from you or something is not permitted, you gain nothing by *not* partaking of it. Where alcohol is forbidden, for example, you would tend to find more alcoholics. Where it is not, you would tend to find less abuse. This is just plain, human nature.

So in this planetary school, those incarnating as the dark brethren also possess free will and are given the prerogative to try again and again to make their choice between right and wrong. He is never condemned to this status forever, for in the light of God's Love, he always has the right to choose the Path of Righteousness. It may take aeons but eventually that soul will come into line with the Path. Many of the bright spiritual lights of today have at one time been part of these Dark Forces and have since chosen the path of light. Some of today's mediums have also experienced a past lifetime or two as black magicians.

Despite their dastardly deeds that often make life on earth an ordeal, the Dark Forces are still creations of God, albeit souls which have chosen the path of ignorance.

## Atlantean Themes of The Dark Forces

The Dark Forces on earth today are the same dropout souls from more advanced evolutions that hijacked the Atlantean civilization centuries before. They have been waiting in the dark wings of the astral plane until earth's present civilization again reached a similar level of Atlantis at the time they destroyed it. Although some may have chosen the path of the light in the meantime, many of them chose to reincarnate on earth to continue their activities in two major areas: 1) the accumulation of money to control the mass of humanity and 2) warmongering as a means of forcing an agenda of oppression on people while generating more monetary gain. Both these Atlantean techniques are ultimately used to prevent or thwart mankind's spiritual re-evolution to its Creator.

Going back about 24,000 years ago, we find Atlantis, a rather sophisticated community and culture at a similar juncture in evolution as earth today, that is, transiting from the Piscean to the Aquarian Age. At that point, Atlanteans had attained a higher level of knowledge in science and technology than earth today. On the spiritual level, however, if we were to take a spiritual poll of the citizenry of Atlantis at that time, we would find that today's souls on earth are much farther along in spiritual attainment than those of Atlantis. This is because every great spiritual luminary in earth's history has most likely reincarnated during these times to play a role in the coming events.

On the scientific-technological level, Atlanteans had discovered the power of sound that could be used in a similar manner to our laser beam technology today. Furthermore, they discovered that sound could be used for military purposes. By aiming sound waves at any organ in the body, they could cause it to explode. Many scientists wanted to experiment and develop this technology so that it could be "tuned" to cause great harm to their enemies.

A great controversy arose over this matter. Although in the Atlantean society, men and women stood on equal footing, this controversy caused a great rift between the two sexes. Women, functioning then as they do now as the conscience of humanity, disagreed with the men who thrilled at pursuing this line of research merely to see just how far they could carry it. In the end, the men prevailed.

Meanwhile, the leaders of the Atlantean financial capitals discovered that by accumulating huge sums of money and driving the majority of the common people into poverty, they could better control them to do their bidding. Not long thereafter, the leaders of both the scientific and the financial communities discovered that by combining high-tech military technology with huge fortunes of money, they could dominate the whole of civilization. Ultimately, this marriage between money and warmongering brought down the Atlantean civilization.

Many of these soul-shells have re-embodied on earth over the past centuries, practicing what they do best as despotic monarchs and emperors, monopolizing power and resources to wage war. One need only refer to world history books to read about the succession of empires and their wars. Presently, they have adapted to the democratic government systems of today and to our civilization's communications technology to again accumulate huge wealth and power. Rather than being limited to certain geographical areas, as in the past, their activities stretch worldwide without respect to nationality, country or race, in effect, fulfilling the prophecy of the hydra-headed monster in the Book of Revelations.

These benighted ones constitute today's form of The Dark Forces. They have embodied in human forms of all races and gender and consistent with their past, they constitute a *genre* of souls which know how to amass huge fortunes of money, to wage wars for further gain, and to control the masses with the aim of stifling their soul evolution. They have been able to deflect these blatant themes by generating every conceivable sophism among intellectuals and practitioners— economic determinism, conservatism, liberalism, communism, capitalism, and the like—to justify or cloak their actions. However, stripped of whatever "ism" they operate under, we see at the very root of all the conflict and strife on planet earth these dual themes of money accumulation and warmongering.

## Waves of Incarnations from the Astral Plane

Just on the other side of death lies the astral plane. Here vast arrays of discarnate beings that have passed through the portal of death reside. These individuals still possess what is considered a material body, only in a more ethereal form, a lighter matter vibrating at a faster rate than our dense physical bodies.

As in the rest of the universe, the astral plane is divided hierarchically into various levels, and discarnates congregate according to their respective levels of spiritual development. They continue to live, work, and study toward their spiritual advancement just as they did in the physical body, only there is no need for money as everything they want is merely thought into existence. Here they review over and over again the mistakes they made during their previous incarnation, and with the help of higher beings, design a reincarnation that will balance out the wrongs and teach new lessons on the physical earth plane.

Passing through the portal of death does not make instant angels out of the dead. A discarnate arrives on the astral plane at exactly the same level of spiritual evolution as when it was in the incarnate. So on the astral plane, there are discarnates who are both the good and bad, but with one big difference–they are not mixed together as they are on earth. Those of similar spiritual dispositions are grouped together: the good and benevolent discarnates band together, while the discarnates of The Dark Forces congregate in their own domain.

What defines the difference between these two groups is: 1) the good are still connected to their Higher Selves or souls and continue to work on their spiritual growth. Guides and teachers from the Great Brotherhood of Light continue to lead this group upward in its spiritual evolution. 2) the benighted discarnates or those of other evolutions, which we cited above, have disconnected from their souls and thus do not follow the Path of evolution. They could thus be called *insane*, although they can decide at any time to reconnect with their souls and continue their spiritual evolution. Many do not and therefore never evolve further than the astral plane. They languish there together, often bored with each others' malevolent company and await another opportunity to incarnate on earth.

Bad company begets more bad company. Imagine an array of unrepentant discarnate beings, the likes of

# The Dark Forces Today

Hitler, Stalin, Mussolini, Hirohito, Franco, Salazar, Trujillo, Mao and Kim Il Song in the company of a host of other minor dictators, thieves, and criminals, biding their time and chomping at the bit to reincarnate!

So just when the earth thinks it has rid itself of a crazed dictator or oppressive monarch or has executed a serial killer, this same being can reincarnate in another human body and continue to cause harm and conflict on earth. They can choose to reincarnate as an infant but in these days, this process might be too slow. It is conceivable that they choose to "walk in" to a body whose soul wants to leave or simply possess an individual entirely. In these days of insanity, such takeovers are entirely possible, although exceptional.

We can see that even if these benighted ones have been executed by the criminal justice system or shot or killed in another circumstance, they can still exercise a certain amount of mischief and evil from the astral plane. This is why the criminal justice systems on both the national and international levels have been unable to stem the tide of crime and conflict. And it seems to get worse and worse with each passing generation.

## Telepathic Influence on Earth

Those benighted ones, unable to find an adequate vehicle of embodiment on earth can project further mischief from where they are onto the earth plane! A certain pent-up frustration develops, for they have no one to torment and victimize among their bad discarnate company. Tormenting themselves would be too boring, for their insanity drives them to spread as much harm and dissension as possible. They instead look for agents or receptive individuals on the earth plane to influence telepathically.

Who, then, becomes their prey on the earth plane? First and most obvious are those incarnate beings of The Dark Forces who have managed to incarnate in locations throughout the world. Second, uneducated psychics who are open to the discarnate's flattery and who communicate with any and every "spirit" voice. Third, the naturally intuitive and clairvoyant, who thrill at communicating with another dimension, not realizing the potential danger of the contact. Fourth, persons of weak character who are prone to certain obsessions or habits such as drugs and alcohol and lose control of their physical faculties. Fifth, the weak-minded whom these astral forces possess and force to commit heinous crimes in the name of God or on their behalf. Sixth, the criminally prone young souls who are easily manipulated to commit a lot of dirty work for The Dark Forces to gain quick riches and power.

The Dark Forces on the earth plane are masters of black magic. Through telepathy they can broadcast or control individuals who are working for them or who are too weak to resist them. These black magicians are programmed to speak the same vocabulary as the workers of good and many take positions in charitable organizations both of a religious or governmental nature.

Just as some of us respond to guidance from spiritual guides or Masters in the Great Brotherhood of Light, the embodied agents of The Dark Forces are also programmed to follow commands emanating from their "colleagues" still on the astral plane. Highly emotional in character, they respond to urgings from the astral plane like automatons and often without realizing it, they are manipulated according to plans The Dark Forces have laid out to oppose the Divine Plan.

## Disseminating Confusion

We have seen that The Dark Forces can communicate telepathically with the emotional bodies of individuals and spur them on to carry out their evil orders From the astral or lower mental planes. Yet the Masters of the Brotherhood also communicate telepathically to humanity but from the higher mental and spiritual planes. From either source, all messages must eventually filter down first through the human subconscious mind, and then through the brain, before the individual takes cognizance of them. And this is where the problem lies: The untrained minds of the mass of humanity cannot distinguish the telepathic messages coming from The Dark Forces from those sent by the Brotherhood.

The Dark Forces' astral waves, often in coordination with the earth's mass media, can easily sway people in one direction or the other. Concurrently, the Brotherhood beams its messages of love and wisdom through this smoke of negativity—in a constant battle to neutralize them. This often accounts for the "tug and pull" that goes on in humanity, for they swing from one extreme position to the other.

It takes the trained esoteric mind to reject the misleading messages of The Dark Forces and seize upon only those sweet messages of wisdom that flow from the upper spiritual planes from the Brotherhood and hold them untouched and unswayed by the media.

## Earth Plane Agents

Conspiracy theories abound about a powerful group of financiers that exercise such control on world affairs from behind the scenes that even duly elected governments succumb as mere puppets of their benighted will. For years, people only whispered stories of the Seven

Sisters, the Illuminati, the Trilateral Commission, the Council on Foreign Relations and the like, all of which purported to wield enough power so as to bring any government, democratic or autocratic, under its influence. The primary purpose of these secret societies is to bring about a One World Government that would subject the whole earth to its dark rule.

All these stories, sounding more like grist for a science fiction novel, are unfortunately true to some extent. However, we should elucidate one fact for your attention: if any of these suspected groups are known to the public by any name whatsoever, you can be certain that they are but front organizations for more sinister and hidden forces who walk about in the halls of the Geneva's money counting houses. They are creations to distract and mislead the public into thinking they can identify The Dark Forces, while the real ones are spinning their ignorance and bad works under different guises.

The earth plane incarnates of The Dark Forces appear as human beings who live and work among us on earth. Those at the top of their hierarchy are fully conscious that they are part of The Dark Forces hierarchy. They inhabit the luxurious palaces of Geneva and other large urban centers in the world, wear the finest suits that money can buy, dine in the finest restaurants, and wear the finest perfumes. Highly intelligent, attractive, and seductive, their influence passes into the highest ranks of governments in the world.

Their influence is so pervasive that an order to transfer funds can cause the stock market to rally one day or to plunge the next. A brief note to the president of a country can start a war with whatever victim country is available. No power structure on earth is without their influence, and they are placed all over the world. And over the years their puppets have come to occupy the highest offices in government and the private sector to make access to legitimate power easier. It is not below them to mimic the work of Great Brotherhood of Light, speaking the same words but using instead black magic phenomena to impress the pliable and dormant minds of the mass of humanity as to their validity and sincerity. Moreover, they have developed telepathic abilities to communicate with their sort all over the world and with their cohorts on the astral plane. Through these abilities, they often impress the media to spread mass discontent and conflict, and mass hysteria is often the result. They even pose as God, sending messages from the astral plane to various religious groups on the earth plane, so that they receive contradictory and conflicting answers to their prayers in the name of God. They have been behind all the religious battles and conflicts the world has known.

They are obsessed with the accumulation of vast sums of money in order to control all aspects of human society. They control the financial and banking systems, governmental taxation and regulatory agencies, the military, stock markets, capital markets, gambling casinos, and public corporations from which they have managed to draw in vast sums of money in every country all over the world. They promote warmongering as a source of further revenue, for the manufacture of war materiel is a lucrative business. In addition, wars stir up fears and dependence among the combatant populations so that they are docile and easy to control. The result is suppression of the rights of the individual.

These malevolent beings or throwbacks from the Atlantean period are organized in a hierarchy much like organized crime. However, their hierarchical structure straddles both the astral and earth planes, which gives them a wider and more flexible field of operation. It also reflects the stymied evolutionary state of their benighted members, for the light and inspiration that come from the higher spiritual planes are blocked.

These benighted ones embody in all races and gender. To understand the depth and breadth of their power, we must lift our thinking above the concept of nationality or the nation-state. We cannot think in terms of American versus Swiss versus English versus Chinese or any such national identity, for The Dark Forces exist without allegiance to any country. National boundaries are completely arbitrary, for they view nations as pawns, useful for pitting one against the other for their gain. Even though America has become their most desirable country to promote their insanity, we still cannot really say The Dark Forces are American, although America unfortunately seems to be its major proponent, instigator, and even victim.

They regard the Cosmic Law of Free Will with disdain, and often use force or telepathic manipulation to impose or possess weak recipients to carry out their agenda. This accounts for periodic waves of criminal activity we encounter on earth—a spat of school shootings, a rash of child abductions with no apparent connection, random sniper killings, infanticide by unsuspecting mothers, irrational domestic jealousies, and murders, terrorist attacks--all carried out by weak or criminally inclined individuals responding to evil broadcasts from The Dark Forces on the astral plane. Most of these perpetrators often cannot account for why they have committed these heinous crimes because they were in reality possessed. Our legal systems call it "temporary insanity."

# The Dark Forces Today

The Dark Forces employ powerful black magicians who are capable of astral travel, that is, leaving the body and traveling to places outside their body, and telekinetic mesmerism, to manipulate machines of any sort–buses, planes, production lines, satellites, and the like—so that they go haywire from any place where these Dark Forces are operating. This accounts for rashes of plane crashes that seem periodically to happen all at once.

Some of these broadcast orders are often so powerful, those caught in the line of fire, for example those of weak mental capacities, under stress, or suffering from mental imbalance also begin to act in a kill mode. These poor individuals, often innocent and without premeditated malice, walk into these broadcast orders and are led to commit some of the most heinous crimes that their original natures would never do. And when they awake, they often do not have any recollection of their evil deeds.

The Dark Forces thus are primarily a negative force that uses mental telepathic means, counter to the positive and uplifting mental impressions from the Great Brotherhood of Light. They appear as intellectually advanced persons all the way down to the petty street criminal. Their ultimate bid to accumulate money and control humanity is dead-ended, a virtual *cul de sac*, but what can be expected from such a benighted group? Such a simplistic and unenlightened goal has nevertheless been devastating for earth at its present stage of evolution.

## Creating Sheep out of Mankind

You might ask, how it is that The Dark Forces have gained so much control on the earth? By design, these Dark Forces have chosen to embody *en masse* at this opportune point in earth's evolution: Good and innocent souls on earth have reached a stage of their cosmic evolution where they must decide whether to govern themselves or let others govern them. The Dark Forces have taken advantage of this quandary to herd those who still feel they need to be governed like sheep and are all too willing to do whatever the status quo dictates regardless of who is dictating it to them. The Dark Forces have in essence, found ready victims among today's incarnations, who are willing to give up their sovereignty and be controlled.

Television became the marvelous invention in the postwar years. Its presence in the lives of mankind has been phenomenal, so that one or many sets can be found in almost everyone's home. Even in the remotest places on earth, one can see people gathered around the television set being entertained in a café, the central square or in a neighbor's home. Now, with satellite broadcasting blanketing the earth, no place need be without television.

From our perspective, these invisible signals from broadcasting stations all over the world reach into each and every household every second of the day. Yet, far beyond the innocent signals beaming reruns of "I Love Lucy," are those that are electronically calibrated to cause varying degrees of retardation, autism, stupidity, mesmerism, and a general sense of malaise in those billions of watchers. This is why you must often make a willful effort to pull yourself away from the television set. People often jokingly refer to being "glued" to the television sets. A better way to put it would be "mesmerized" by their television sets.

Turn off your television set. Hang a piece of string in front of the screen. Turn the set on again, and you will observe the string jump forward as the rays from the set enter the room. Again, these signals have been calibrated to numb and placate you and the more hours you and your children spend watching television, the more you are susceptible to its deleterious effects, among which are to render you lax, lazy, and unable to think clearly.

In addition to these electronic signals, television programming caters to the emotional rather than the rational thought processes of mankind, often at the level of the lowest common denominator. People today tend to react emotionally and television programs often appeal to the emotions of their viewers. Programs depict characters, often beautiful and attractive on the outside, but who are not in control of their emotions. Watch these programs objectively. The popular ones are full of people screaming at each other. Somebody is losing his or her temper. Somebody is cheating. Everybody is in violation of cosmic law, over and over and over again. Unfortunately, these are the programs people find the most interesting.

Hardly can you view a program where a brave soul is pitted against a wonderful set of obstacles and spiritually overcomes them all. We see very few, if any, victories of that type portrayed. Instead, you find people constantly involved in the most intricate and convoluted relationships with one other, invariably in violation of cosmic law. It is as if someone were trying to say, "This is who you are, this is what you are. Accept it. This is your lot. You're a bunch of squabbling animals and you'll not be anything more than that." For according to cosmic law, what you place your attention upon is what you become. What man meditates upon he eventually becomes.

Television is also used to divert public opinion away from mischief. A few years ago the world was kept riveted to their television sets carrying the trial of an individual by the name of O.J. Simpson. For months they watched and heard the blow-by-blow accounts of Mr. Simpson and whether he did or did not kill his wife. How interesting? What else might have been occurring while people were being distracted? In the U.S., a missing Congressional aide who had an affair with a U.S. Congressman gripped the American public in the days leading up to the attack on the World Trade Center in New York.

The majority of mankind, glued to their television have in effect ceded the God-given right to think, create, and experiment to outside forces. The deleterious effects of the well-calibrated electronic signals reaching into the living quarters of almost every family on earth and the humanly demeaning programming have such a numbing effect on humanity that The Dark Forces are able to sway the public in one direction or the other, march them into war, herd them to their own executions, and take their hard-earned money right out from under their noses.

## Recognizing Individuals of the Dark Forces

Listen to what your business and government leaders say and discern what is really going on. The words of wisdom left us by the Master Jesus, "By their fruits ye shall know them" applies most poignantly here.

Some of you serving in the vanguard of the Brotherhood may find yourselves in the unfortunate situation of being in the presence of such beings. You will note the marked absence of anything that could remotely be called human emotion, sentiment, and certainly love. Like robots, they have no souls, for they are simply energy units programmed to control this planet in human form, thus they are not wholly human as you would define human. One could say that they possess the same mindset of a serial killer who thinks nothing of killing one, two, three, four, five, six up to fifty or more people and would continue doing the same, unless stopped. As leaders of any power, they can summarily order the slaughter of hundreds or thousands of individuals without flinching. What kind of being can do this? Certainly not the type of human being you would associate with willingly, for his conscious mind, the so-called daily working state of mind, is separated from the super-conscious mind or Higher Self. So, by definition this being is insane.

Where do these beings operate? In the next two chapters, we shall cover more details about the two worlds of The Dark Forces: money accumulation and warmongering. Their cohorts exist more or less in these two lines of activities in all sectors and all levels of society.

Every day we read in the newspapers about violent individuals, perpetrators of violence, thieves, embezzlers, and the like. These are the obvious ones who pepper our society with their mischief, and at the same time, divert our attention from the huge crimes against humanity and their directors who remain unseen.

Those who direct these activities on the earth plane remain behind a thick veil of secrecy and move about the financial capitals of the world unrecognized and imperceptible to the common people. They meet in the great halls of Geneva to plot and plan wars for gain and conceive of schemes for taking people's money, as if it were a game.

They do not belong to any particular country, nationality, or race. In fact, they view national borders as petty obstacles they can easily surmount through the advent of electronic money transfers and a complex nexus of multi-level contacts. They populate an international network of banking and financial institutions, top ranks of government, the military, the military industrial complex, and the diplomatic services. They move in circles that best promote their fluid and mobile existence, passing across borders unannounced and transferring huge sums of money to undisclosed places.

These hidden controllers of the financial system of this planet also have their counterparts: the promoters of the virtue of poverty. Many groups preach the rejection of money and the virtue of the poor. Some convince their followers, like so many sheep, to give up all their worldly belongings in favor of a movement while their leaders build, in the name of the movement, a more than comfortable life for themselves.

They occupy high offices in the traditional church hierarchies. Many of the sect leaders are of such a breed. They parrot the religious and sanctimonious outer coverings to deceive the onlooker into thinking they are indeed souls of the good and angelic type. But you will also note that they are often illogical when speaking of good because they cannot think very deeply of it.

In the war-making business, The Dark Forces manage from afar industrial enterprises of weaponry and so-called defense contractors, never exposing themselves to scrutiny by directly managing such enterprises.

Curiously, their warmongering activities also have a counterpart, and that is the peace movement. Today, this has manifested as the Pan-Anti movements. Although many good and innocent souls belong to these movements, many of the active leaders might be called agents of The Dark Forces, for they promote division and spew hatred against symbols or icons of warmongering who are not necessarily the real perpetrators of war. This is often done to divert the public's attention away from the real perpetrators. For example, peace movements often burn in effigy figures of leaders they think are

## The Dark Forces Today

promoting war, whereas they are but puppets of the real planners and makers of war.

The medical profession has also come under the influence of The Dark Forces. Rather than healers, we now have those who merely seek to make a lot of money. This accounts for the exorbitantly high price for medical services in the United States and the lack of any national health service for American citizens.

There is also a whole population of pressure groups. Many mouth the virtues of the services and movements, which they quietly sabotage. Sometimes the loudest advocates of peace and anti-globalization movements are essentially divisive, and promote the "we-they" syndrome and uncompromising solutions. The environmental movement has become such a victim. The good that could come out of such a movement is tied up in a nexus of regulatory red tape, so as to render it ineffective.

There are also those who mouth truths in the occult movements. They purport to represent this and that Master, using innocent psychics to convey their twisted and distorted versions of the truth. Their shallowness is often revealed as they chant mantras but show no deep understanding. They are disconnected from their souls, automatons programmed to act in the name of good.

Incarnates of The Dark Forces are often highly intelligent and physically attractive, exuding a certain material magnetism or charisma that enables them to draw in people. They have accessed the top ranks of world organizations or sit on boards of directors as the power behind the throne. As we stated above, they inhabit the financial and banking systems of the world, bourses and stock markets, tax collection agencies of government, corporate enterprises (public ones of huge dimensions and by nature hard to scrutinize) and basically any organization that takes in money through contributions such as political parties, charity organizations, and religious organizations.

The clerics in the Muslim religious orders who advocate the holy Jihad wars are not consciously aware of their connection with the Dark Forces yet, they have been put there as receptors to these telepathic orders. Their position in the earthly religious hierarchy affords them much power and influence, and they are able to press the buttons of hatred at will, all of course justifying their actions by scripture. When the mesmeric orders are sent forth or directed at them, they often react as if they have seen a religious vision, one of course that justifies even further the righteousness of their heinous actions.

Leaders in the supposedly free Western Democracies, who gain their official positions through election or appointments of the elected, are also susceptible to the influences of The Dark Forces. It would be unfair to say that all those who have been elected are agents of The Dark Forces, although there are many in the rank and file who receive advice from them in the back rooms of power. Rarely, do you find a member of The Dark Forces as a very public political figure exposed to public scrutiny in an election. What you are likely to see is the politician-puppet of anonymous influences behind the scenes.

Elections are the playgrounds of The Dark Forces. An electoral candidate, who covets the position to a great degree, is readily compromised, and often "sells his soul to the devil." The narrower the results of a primary election, the more vulnerable the candidate is to those influences that arrive at the last minute to guarantee him the election. All elections are closely watched in the halls of The Dark

Forces.

The Dark Forces have been here on the planet for generations, and yet, they sense the forces of light are about to interrupt their lucrative activities. Although it does not appear so, they are "on the run." Like fleeing desperados who rape and pillage before defeat, The Dark Forces are going in for the kill during these final days and years.

But fortunately, cosmic law will not allow them this destiny. Their reign on earth is destined to end and due to cosmic cycles, a grand new awakening at the grassroots level, of which you, the reader, are a part, will ultimately awaken people to the point where they will start to question things. And just like the French peasants in the French Revolution, they will storm the Bastille and shout, "Enough! Enough! Off with their heads!"

# CHAPTER 4
## Control of the Nation-State

In the post World War II era, the world was divided into three major zones: 1) the so-called free world, 2) the communist bloc, and 3) the third world of non-aligned nations. In each of the three zones, the Dark Forces have adopted different methods to carry out their Atlantean legacy of money accumulation and warmongering.

In the Soviet bloc, the Stalinist party dictatorships created government bureaucracies that monopolized all sectors of the economies in their Baltic, East European, Balkan, Central Asian, and East Asian satellite states. The Communist Party drained money and resources from their populations and spent huge sums on their militaries. These party dictatorships were the starkest examples of the reincarnation of the Atlantean model of money accumulation and warmongering.

In the non-aligned world, there were also egregious examples of the Atlantean governance that exacerbated the already impoverished post war conditions. For the most part, these third world nations adopted less centralized Socialist "republic" models that tended to impoverish their nations through the voracious appetites of their bureaucracies and gave rise to strongmen leaders, often military men, who were surrounded by a favored class of sycophant businesses and extended family members. Again wealth was concentrated in the hands of the favored class, while the government spent much on the army (as opposed to their navies and air force) because the armies could be used to oppress the people and engage their immediate neighboring countries in war. So in the third world we see the same Atlantean themes playing out: concentration of money in the hands of a few and warmongering.

In the so-called free world of western democracies, the Atlantean themes have also been played out in subtler ways. The famous arms race with the Communist Bloc resulted in huge military expenditures and many wars such as: the Korean, Nicaraguan, Lebanese, Israeli-Palestinian, Cuban, Vietnam, and Iraqi conflagrations, to name a few.

These western countries loudly promoted free trade on their terms, often violating these principles when convenient. Through trade agreements and control of the international finance system that governed the terms of trade, they engaged most of the non-aligned countries and to a very limited extent the communist bloc in commerce. With virtually no competition from a massive portion of the globe, the Soviet Bloc and China, the western nations traded freely with the rest of the world. The result was a massive accumulation of wealth in the western democracies and an unprecedented technological modernization of western society, primarily in material well-being.

Working in democratic nations as opposed to the more blatant forms in the communist and non-aligned worlds, The Dark Forces had to devise subtler methods to bring this massive wealth under their control. In this and the following chapters, we shall elicit how The Dark Forces were able to engineer the largest transfer of wealth in all the history of mankind through their control of taxes, the national debts, and the stock markets.

Many would say, "My life is so simple. Why should I be bothered with The Dark Forces?" Then there is the old saying, "The only two things certain in life are taxes and death." If you pay any kind of tax, you are touched by The Dark Forces.

The Dark Forces bring their sophisticated ability to attract and accumulate huge sums of money from their days as Atlanteans. Their general strategy is to accumulate the major part of the world's wealth in their corner, then leverage this financial power to control mankind. The obvious sources of money accumulation are national governments, which by fiat or decree, have the ability to take money from their citizens under the threat of force.

## Hijacking Tax Revenue

Governments today like the feudal lords of yore have the right to tax or, to put it bluntly, to force their citizens to pay taxes. A citizen pays taxes ostensibly to support law enforcement in the society, build and maintain the communications and transport infrastructures, regulate utilitarian services such as the post office, air transport, defend of his society from outside incursions, and pay a host of other expenses the government incurs. Some functions of government are without question for the common good of its citizens, yet some are highly questionable. Yet most citizens never question the validity of ever-increasing taxes and willingly pay their taxes as a civic duty.

## Control of the Nation-State

Governments on all levels of society impose taxes on every aspect of life to support their ever-increasing demand for revenue. For instance, they levy taxes on gasoline, cigarettes, alcohol, luxury goods, travel, schools, water, heating oil, airport security, border security, port charges, customs, sales taxes, surtaxes on taxes, value-added taxes, air travel, the food you eat at restaurants—in other words, on just about everything you pay for to survive. Even retirees, the sick and infirm, the lame and disabled must pay taxes on their living stipends. In fact, governments extract surreptitiously so much cash from its populations that the average citizen must borrow money to make ends meet. Private lending agencies extend credit in the form of personal and equity loans, credit cards, and consumer credit that indebt the weary taxpayer to some external organization. They will even lend the citizen money to pay annual income taxes!

In the United States, where taxes are constitutionally mandated as voluntary, the agency charged with collecting tax revenues, the Internal Revenue Service, was created surreptitiously and by design without any legal mandate. Yet today, operating on a very questionable mandate, it collects billions of dollars in taxes with the help of armed police cadres who will throw citizens in jail if they do not pay. The IRS has a murky legal status which keeps its activities outside the purview of the law. Yet, it promulgates tax rules and regulations under the threat of force. Further research into the tax collection functions in other countries in the world should reveal similar arrangements.

Whether the tax revenue service in the country is legal or not is one matter but all these agencies share one common characteristic: they are inviolable and <u>never</u>

audited. In other words, taxpaying citizens never know exactly the amount their tax collection agencies <u>really</u> take in. The fact that huge sums are appropriated for covert activities under the guise of national security but do not appear on the national budget or are never publicly acknowledged, indicates but the tip of the iceberg of this egregious situation. Every citizen of the world should be asking the question: **How much taxes is my country really collecting?**

To confuse the taxpayer and obfuscate this situation, complex tax regulations make it virtually impossible for any private watchdog organization to calculate the amount the government receives in tax revenue. "There is an exception to every regulation. We consider each taxpayer on a case by case basis," the tax service will say. This is why any effort to simplify the tax code and adopt a straight universal tax rate for everyone, meets with such opposition. A straight tax would make it too easy for the citizens to figure out how much money the tax system is really collecting.

Worldwide tax collecting agencies have positioned themselves to collect not only billions, but trillions of dollars, every single year from citizens. And to aid them further, the World Bank has recently funded a one billion dollar project to render tax revenue systems in developing countries even more efficient to collect taxes! However efficient these tax collections services become, they are never accountable to anyone for how much they take in. Published figures of tax revenue come from the tax revenue service, not from any independent third party verification. What those in the government tax services really do with the funds is never reported.

But one thing is certain, from our perspective, they fatten their own pockets, at the expense of their citizenry.

The U.S reputedly the richest and most powerful nation in the world has yet to create a viable national health system to care for its citizens. Yet, it spends billions on the military and space programs and much more on covert activities.

The general public must wake up and question all taxes paid. Of course, there are dissidents who rail against these injustices but compared to the vast majority of people, who follow along like so many sheep led to the slaughter, they are but a very small minority. Each one of us should mentally cry out every time the cash register in the store tacks on a sales tax or TVA and ask, "Wait a minute! Where is this money going? Why should we pay it?" This mental resistance invokes energy from the spiritual dimensions that loosen the grip taxes now hold on the world.

Individuals should ask their government representatives if they know the exact amount of revenue their government takes in through taxes. But do not be surprised if you meet with a blank face. Has anyone ever thought of asking this question? Furthermore, ask them if an independent auditor outside the government has ever audited the tax revenue agency. You don't have to carry signs and demonstrate in front of your tax collection agencies. Simply asking these pertinent questions does immeasurable good at loosening the grip The Dark Forces have on the world's money supply. It invokes not only the power of your Higher Self but the resources of the Brotherhood to correct this situation in another dimension, for once this is done, the solution manifests here on the earth plane. Your questions and probes will have a snowball effect in bringing this egregious situation to the surface.

## Bureaucracy: Funneling Tax Revenues

No one dares to subject any bureaucracy in the world to a serious cost-benefit analysis, for the foregone conclusion would be that the cost of maintaining them far exceeds any benefits derived from them. We all know deep down that government bureaucracies waste money, but when faced with the prospect of challenging these behemoths, we usually just sink back and try not to think of it. In the meantime, our taxes increase as bureaucracies grow. Economists and financial analysts just throw up their hands and call the burden of maintaining government bureaucracies a "sunk cost" or something we must tolerate.

This is understandable, because these inventions are like steamrollers that cannot be stopped and are designed to: 1) concentrate huge sums of money in one place and 2) spend huge sums of money without producing any themselves. They serve as one-way funnels through which money is passed and provides the sole justification for taxation, for without them no one could justify the systematic, forced taxation that pervades our whole planet.

A government bureaucratic organization touches in some way or the other every person. Its tentacles reach into every person's pocket, 24 hours a day, to satisfy its insatiable appetite for money. There is a tax on everything you consume, even the air you breathe and the water you drink. Year after year, rarely does the operating budget of a bureaucracy decrease. Although at times it may remain at the same level, in the end while public attention is diverted, these budgets always increase.

So by its very nature, a bureaucratic organization is parasitic, for it cannot produce anything but paper and regulations. Some create licenses, permits, identification cards, certificates, and the like to generate more cash in addition to their tax allotted budget. Some have even instituted express services, so that they can charge a premium price for their services, much like the under-the-table payments bureaucrats take in some countries "to facilitate" hurdling the barriers they themselves have created.

Since they operate under an official capacity, government agencies can commandeer the news media. Government officials constantly praise themselves with laudatory speeches to justify the services their particular agencies are rendering to the public. They must constantly remind the people how much good they are doing for them.

On the grassroots level, small local government services are vital to maintaining a certain order in the society. On the national level, however, their justifications are highly questionable, for it is only on these upper levels—provincial or state, national and international—that the most expensive and solidly institutionalized forms of bureaucracy exist, for they are farthest from public scrutiny. Citizens can keep a hawk eye on their local government workers but they are helpless to scrutinize bureaucracies on the state, provincial, national, and international levels.

On all issues facing mankind today, the bureaucratic mindset injects a general paralysis into the decision-making process so that its self-preservation is always considered above all other issues on the table. It is hierarchy gone amuck, a complete distortion of the original idea. Most bureaucratic institutions begin with lofty ideals and a certain vibrancy and optimism.

Gradually the organizations' self-interest creeps in. Salaries, medical benefits, retirements, travel and education perks become its primordial concern. Low risk and the preservation of their jobs color the thinking of the bureaucrat, and rarely does one find there is one brave enough to stake his position on principle.

The public complains constantly about "the bureaucrats," their cost, their inefficiency, and their burgeoning growth, yet bureaucracies continue to dominate our lives and grow– despite the harm they might be doing to the citizenry of the world. Why is this? The answer is plain and simple: they were not created to serve humanity. They were, established to serve the interests of The Dark Forces.

**Bureaucratization of the World**

The post-WWII years saw an exponential burgeoning of bureaucratic organizations. Those giants, China and Russia, which turned to Communism, created massive totalitarian government structures and civil services that literally controlled all activities of the country and every aspect of the common man's life. The spread of communism into East Europe, the Balkans, the Baltic States, North Korea, North Vietnam, and Cuba resulted in massive bureaucracies for even the smallest of countries.

Added to this trend were the democratic socialist movements in Europe that created more social and health services, government parastatals, semi-public enterprises, and new layers of bureaucracy on top of the traditional ones in a bid to meld capitalism and socialism. The result was the development of even larger bureaucratic governments trying to govern and engage in commerce.

During the 1950s and 1960s, National Liberation Fronts fought to free British, French, Spanish, Dutch and

Portuguese colonies from their metropolitan colonial masters and created a host of new countries in Asia, South Asia, and Africa. These countries, imbued with Leninist anti-imperialist ideology, tended to adopt large government bureaucracies according to the socialist or communist models. Ponderous bureaucracies grew out of countries barely able to feed their own populations.

In the countries of the so-called free world, federal, state, provincial and local bureaucracies grew at an unprecedented pace. On the national level, the Cold War increased the need to maintain large military establishments, while citizens demanded more government regulatory intervention into every facet of life. So light laissez-faire governments took on more and more, the ponderous heavy bureaucracies of the rest of the world.

As if these ponderous national governments were not enough, the post war euphoria elicited idealism that a new era of world peace was at hand. War-weary nations formed the United Nations system, a supranational nexus of political, social, cultural, agricultural, banking, investment banking, financial and technical regulatory agencies that sought to blanket the world with more redundant bureaucracy. To make matters worse, each region set up regional supranational organizations such as the Organization of American States, the Organization of African States, the Association of Southeast Asian Nations ASEAN, the European Community, etc., all of which added yet another layer of regional international bureaucracy. European citizens, already groaning under the weight of their voracious national government bureaucracies, have created yet another layer in the European Union. And NATO, void of its anti-Soviet

Bloc, has survived by inviting new members, some of them former Soviet Bloc countries, to join in an even bigger, more costly, defense organization. In addition to these "official" governmental bureaucracies, charitable organizations of purported goodwill began to sprout up everywhere. The Roman Catholic, Anglican, Episcopal and Baptist church organizations expanded their services worldwide. These religious, nonprofit, and charitable organizations accumulated untold amounts of wealth, all claiming to redistribute a portion to the poor and needy. Some of these organizations stretch around the globe and may, in some cases, be larger than some national governments. The international association for nonprofit organizations in the world lists over twenty thousand of these agencies.

Most bureaucratic organizations were founded on certain principles or ideals. Yet once established and well anchored into a system of government, The Dark Forces infiltrated them and sabotaged any initial idealism that may have existed. The United Nations is probably the best example. The result has been to neutralize these organizations, rendering them bloated, useless and ineffective, while draining the worldwide resources of a starving world.

## Mischief in Huge Bureaucracies

Most bureaucratic organizations consist of three levels of employees. The top tier of managers and leaders is where The Dark Forces operate. Often ambitious, yet posing as managers for the common good, they channel tax revenues accorded them to support the ongoing maintenance of the bureaucracy and secondarily, the bureaucracy's programs. They live a fine life of chauffeur-driven cars, private planes, and mansions and enjoy all the

## Control of the Nation-State

accoutrements of the rich and the privileged. Their status and signature enable them to move trillions of dollars around the world for various purposes.

The second tier of bureaucrats consists of relatively idealistic individuals who provide the technical backbone to the organization. Experts in their respective fields, with good to noble intentions, at least in the beginning, they learn that their ideals have no place in the bureaucracy and their growing cynicism becomes a threat to the top tier. To placate them, management guarantees them a steady salary, job security like no other in the world, seniority, and lifetime retirement benefits. Few on this second level would give up this security to exert their ideals.

The last tier consists of the support and administrative staff. They are the expendable ones, especially during downturns in the economy. The bureaucracy expands and contracts on this level leaving the other levels relatively intact, yet despite this show of contraction from time to time, the overall bureaucracy continues to increase, especially during crises and war.

It is on the top tier where we observe The Dark Forces operating in their stride. They speak the same language and espouse the same pat goals as the rest of their colleagues in the bureaucracy. Ambitious and power-hungry, they grapple to the top and will step on whomever gets in their way. They invariably reach the top. It is also on this level that the secret movement of tax revenue funds takes place, for this is the main underlying purpose of these bureaucracies. The departments, ministries or agencies in charge of foreign policy, international intelligence, the diplomatic service, foreign aid, liaison with the international organizations, all branches of the military, and international commerce of agricultural goods enjoy freedom of movement across borders not accorded to the ordinary citizen. In every government in the world there are equivalent, counterpart agencies, so that there is always a ready contact point. The so-called agreements on diplomatic immunity allow much secrecy– secret budgets, projects and movement of funds– that the public never sees.

While funds move secretly through these "official" channels, the work of the lower two tiers serves as the "storefront" for the bureaucratic organization to the public. When the public makes demands on them for the services they purport to provide, the bureaucrat will often choose to take no action or expend the least amount of energy either to block or drag matters out. Mired in internal, self-imposed regulations and procedures, few have the energy or the desire to surmount all the obstacles to serve the public.

As bureaucratic decrees accord more and more perks, the comfortable bureaucrat seeks more and more to preserve what he has. The bureaucracy's survival thus becomes its primary goal. Salaries, fringe benefits, and retirement packages take on greater importance than any lofty service goals to the public. During a severe downturn in the economy, government workers in one state in the U.S. demanded a pay raise regardless of the hardship it would cause on the citizens of the state.

In order to carry out its clandestine acts, it is all too common for the top tier to summarily cut the two lower layers of the bureaucracy off from any relevant communication, thereby creating two separate organizations within the same bureaucracy. The top tier bureaucrats acquire the best of government mansions, ride in expensive cars, hold seminars in expensive country clubs and hotels, travel internationally in private jets, all in the name of service to the people. State affairs are among the most lavish in the world today. Even in some of the least developed countries in the world, caviar and spirits flow among the glitterati, while their impoverished populations peer through the garden gates watching the spectacle of wealth before their eyes.

### Mis-Directed Priorities

Aside from the clandestine expenditures bureaucracies make beyond public scrutiny, they must decide how the governments will spend the tax revenues. Even if their decisions bear the stamp of the Congress or Parliament, it does not mean they reflect the will of the people. It is ironic that the only superpower to emerge out of the Cold War should feel the most threatened by terrorism. The trillions spent on researching, building, and maintaining a high-tech military superstructure, while millions of the planet's inhabitants live on the brink of starvation, defies common logic.

We have regimes here on earth today that keep people in a state of abject poverty so that they are too weak to resist, that is, they control people by depriving them of what money could buy—food, medicines, clothing, housing, fresh water—to meet their basic needs. We also have whole continents of human beings dying from disease and starvation while countries allocate billions of dollars to their space programs to bring back rocks from dead planets near earth with which to experiment.

Yet, when we consider the Atlantean roots from where these priorities come, we can understand that these spending priorities are not meant to serve humanity but instead The Dark Forces.

### Bureaucratic Invention: A Dark Instrument

In the developing countries, where central government plays the chief role in the economic, social and political domains, we already have stark examples of how bureaucracy can literally drain whole countries of their resources and reduce them to vassals of more powerful state nations. A country whose bureaucratic structures depend on foreign aid from another can but do the bidding of the stronger.

Today's developing countries with so little resources to begin with created bureaucratic monsters that impoverished their citizens to the point that even tax collection at gunpoint could not yield any more revenue. At one time, these territories at least produced enough food for their populations. Many now exist primarily on handouts from the developing nations in the form of foreign aid and the balance of payment loans.

A position in the government bureaucracy is blatantly a passport to wealth. Government ministers secretly transfer what's left of their country's wealth or "gifts" of foreign aid into private accounts in Switzerland, while their impoverished countrymen speak in awe at such audacity and wish for the same. Is it not curious that some of the richest individuals in the world come from some of the most impoverished nations on earth? While they live in their palaces, their people struggle to find enough food for the day.

Some countries have been reduced to the point where even the bureaucrats are not paid. However, they retain certain powers so that their fellow citizens must pay them under-the-table gifts to avail themselves of certain government services. The long lines seen across the globe of the poor trying to receive some basic services from their government social agencies is a poignant picture of the complete disregard these bureaucracies have for the welfare of the people they were created to serve. The arrogance of the comfortable bureaucrat as he throws up obstacle after obstacle before the common man seeking relief, paints an even more pathetic picture that these organizations are but alien structures meant to TAKE rather than GIVE.

Seen from a higher perspective, bureaucracies respond not to the pleas of the needy but to power and money in the form of *bakshish, guanxi, fear, or under-the-table payments*. They are instruments that shift money away from the real problems that face the world such as starvation and disease. More recently in the richer nations, manufactured terrorism has struck so much fear in the citizens of each nation that bureaucracies have allocated themselves huge sums of money for security and defense, almost without opposition or resistance from the people, this again, while the basic problems of the world fester.

But all should know that these huge national and international bureaucracies are not a necessary result of mankind's evolution or a necessary response to the modern way of life, as some would like us to believe. They far outstrip the resources consumed—even by the most grandiose of monarchical entourages in the history of mankind. They are in fact, aberrations and distortions of the concept of hierarchy. They are merely dark inventions, the hydra-headed monster referred to in the bible, whose main function is the justification of the ever-growing tax burden and the funnel in which funds are moved to surreptitious destinations.

While earth's problems linger without apparent

solution, the grand bureaucratic structures on earth have created a world of their own. Like parasites, they draw money and resources from mankind, then reallocate the funds to suit their own dark objectives. In a sense, the peoples of the world are paying these bureaucracies to suppress them! So as this cosmic cycle comes to an end, and earth evolves toward its general enlightenment, mankind will hopefully be jolted into mentally resisting the bureaucracies' constant demands and justifications for more taxes, for it is only money that keeps these bureaucracies alive. Deprive them of this life-stream and they will wither away and then a new form of service organization can manifest itself.

By cosmic law, you say "yes," by default "no," if you remain silent. If you do not resist, reject or say "no" to something, then of course you remain tacitly in agreement with it. Yet, there is no need for you to get yourself arrested and thrown into jail in this type of protest. If we are all derivations of the Godhead, we as gods and goddesses can firmly resist The Dark Forces' ploys to take our money, and you will be surprised how powerful your thoughts are to stop them. It is the sleepy mental mindset of sheep-like acceptance that gives them *carte blanche* to do what they will.

## Sell Out of Nations: The National Debt

Most of us at one time have borrowed money. When you buy a house, you often sign a mortgage agreement with a bank or lender that indebts you to them for twenty, maybe thirty years. If you buy a car on credit, you sign a debt for three to five years. Most people try to honor these debts. But if you do not make payments on the mortgage, for instance, the lender will seize the property and throw you out on the streets. If you do not

## Control of the Nation-State 69

make your car payments, the lender will take back the car. So the lender always holds a threat over your head, and you feel an obligation to him.

Today, countries around the world borrow trillions of dollars from unknown lenders. It is only logical to assume that these lenders in turn exercise enormous influence on the leaders of indebted countries, enough influence to render even the president of the most powerful country on earth a mere puppet.

During the Twentieth Century, most nations in the world abandoned the gold standard. This meant it was no longer necessary to back a currency with gold bullion. Instead, nations printed and minted their own money out of paper and other cheaper metals and decreed these instruments to be of value. The nation would support its currency by good fiscal management of the economy and this would give suppliers and consumers the confidence to use paper for commercial exchanges.

More recently, cash as a medium of exchange has become obsolete. Now, commercial exchanges take place using even more ephemeral forms of money, primarily electronic money/ledger transfers or credit/debit cards. This has given money even more fluidity. Huge sums of money can move from one end of the earth to another in a matter of seconds, and when manipulated properly can disappear or reappear at the flick of a switch. The use of cash in the form of paper and coins is left to the masses to conduct their daily transactions, but even on this level, people are using debit and credit cards to purchase even their most basic groceries. In fact, anyone carrying or dealing with too much cash is now branded a money launderer or an illicit dealer of drugs or arms.

Once off the gold standard, governments took

advantage of this less restrictive environment to increase their spending exponentially, for all they had to do was print or mint whatever they needed. As government bureaucracies burgeoned, their operating and program budgets ballooned to the point that these same governments claimed tax revenues could no longer cover their spending requirements. They learned that just printing money to cover these expenses would cause inflation, dilute the value of the currency, and undermine worldwide confidence in the currency.

To cover the yearly budgetary shortfall, governments decided to borrow the money necessary from the financial markets to cover the runaway deficit. The U.S. Government, for example, issued Treasury certificates, long-term notes, bonds, and other ad hoc instruments—promissory notes— to anyone who would lend them money and in return, it would guarantee the lender a good interest payment on the principal. To date, the U.S. Treasury has sold 44 trillion dollars of these instruments on the open markets worldwide and pays a yearly interest of about 400 billion dollars or 1.5 billion dollars per day! And this debt is growing. We use the U.S. as an example because of the size of the debt, but it is certain that every country on earth today is in debt.

During the highly speculative years of the 1990s, government debt instruments were not popular with the most conservative of investors, yet someone was buying up every issue? The U.S. government claims 55 percent of the debt is held by private investors, while the rest is being funded by borrowing from the Social Security Trust Fund. This is only one such case.

While the national leaders have hawked the assets of the country to unknown lenders, they continue to tax the citizens to pay the interest on these loans. Many people shrug their shoulders when confronted with this problem, for it is difficult for them to conceive that a government could go bankrupt, especially if it has the power to tax its citizens by force whenever it needs more funds.

Yet no one seems to ask the most pertinent of questions: TO WHOM IS THE GOVERNMENT INDEBTED? In other words, who are lending the nations of the world trillions and trillions of dollars?

The answering of this simple question will reveal an unimaginable power—The Dark Forces—that owns the assets of your respective countries! And like all lenders, they exert a tremendous bargaining power on the leaders of countries, to do their bidding. One of the most shocking examples of this power is what happened to President Kennedy. For refusing to drag the U.S. into a war with Vietnam, he was summarily executed in broad daylight before the world.

Borrowing money is not free and the government must pay interest on the national debt. To get the money for the interest, the government taxes its citizens, so that each taxpaying citizen is in essence paying an indirect tax (the interest) to The Dark Forces. In the U.S., this debt interest amounts to $3.3 trillion annually.

But even if your governments will never tell you the truth about this situation, we but ask you to stretch your imagination a little further and use a bit of logic. If you were a leader of a country, would you not be beholden to the entity that owned trillions of dollars of your country's debt? The answer is obvious, for calling such a huge debt at any time would cause the immediate collapse of a country's economy!

Today, we have examples of governments in South

America and Africa that are so in debt that they can no longer make their interest payments. They are in effect bankrupt and in their struggle to meet their financial obligations to the lenders, their leaders have literally turned on their own citizens and raided their savings. These countries portend the future of every country that comes under the grip of The Dark Forces, for these will not stop until they have drained each nation of its resources.

Realize that this situation does indeed exist and simply start asking yourselves or your government officials and representatives, "Who really owns the debt of my country? Whenever was the debt made? Why weren't we consulted before you indebted our country, our community?" The answers would startle you, for most would pretend not know.

Yet if you exert your right to merely ask these questions, you invoke the Brotherhood's power to wage a war against this egregious situation in the upper dimensions, then as that battle comes to an end, the veil of ignorance on the earth plane will gradually be lifted and the stranglehold The Dark Forces hold on each nation will be knocked loose. People will wake up and realize the extent of the problem.

It should be apparent to you that any entity that has trillions of dollars to lend the governments of the world must be a formidable force with which to reckon. It should also be clear that these forces hold the world in its grip to the point that they can dictate what course nations must take regardless of what their people want. This is one of the reasons that the United Nations has been rendered useless, for it is not the will of the community of nations that drives things during these times but the will of The Dark Forces. So, is it not surprising that some nations will engage in warfare and not heed the vociferous outcries of the world community to the contrary?

Where do these forces draw their revenue to be able to hold the tremendous debt of the nations? One of the sources we have already cited above—the unreported revenue taken from tax collections. A second source comes from the pillaging of the private sector.

# CHAPTER 5
## Pillaging the Private Sector
*"The more there is of mine, the less there is of yours."*
                                        Alice in Wonderland

We have seen from the above, how it is possible for The Dark Forces to use the threat of force to accumulate huge sums of money through taxes and channel it through "official" government bureaucracies for their own covert uses. They then lend gargantuan sums back to nations and earn billions more in interest. Moreover, they use the national debt to leverage influence on national decisions.

In the past, when despots and monarchs coveted their subjects' property, they either seized it by royal fiat, or if the subject knew what was good for him, he would present it to the king as a gift. In the post-World War II years, one-half of the world fell under Communist dictatorships which summarily seized all property in the name of the people as represented by the state. In essence, national communist parties and their dictators resumed the place of the despots of the past and took what they wanted from the people.

In the Western Democracies, where vast amounts of the world's money became more and more concentrated, the individual's right to own private property and chattel is protected by law and enshrined in the capitalist system, so the Dark Forces could not as easily dispossess people of their property. By working in the so-called free market system, The Dark Forces devised even more ingenious ways to seize people's wealth. Their target was primarily the United States and Western Europe and to a lesser extent, the so-called Tigers of Southeast and East Asia (Taiwan, Hong Kong, Singapore, South Korea, and Thailand) where much of the world's wealth had accumulated.

## Two Crude Oil Shocks

The first major postwar transfer of wealth came in the early 1970s with the oil shock. The despots of the oil-producing countries that grouped under the cartel known as the Organization of Petroleum Exporting Countries (OPEC) forcibly transferred trillions of dollars from all over the world into the Swiss banks– simply by pulling back on production and raising the price of crude oil a few dollars. Most of this transfer came from the western democracies, which were thriving economies at the time. The poorer countries, also dependent on oil, suffered deeply.

To double the pain on the individual consumer, national governments around the world jumped in the act and tacked on huge gas and environmental taxes to the already swollen crude and gasoline prices, ostensibly to discourage people's consumption of and dependence on oil products. Taxes on gasoline account for up to 50 percent of the price of gasoline in some parts of the world and gave governments more tax revenue. It certainly did not discourage oil consumption, for in fact the world's dependence on oil remains at all time highs.

Nevertheless after this first double-punch oil shock, the world gradually adjusted to the higher crude oil prices over a period of twenty-five years and recovered. By 1998, the price of crude had fallen as more non-OPEC producers entered the crude oil market. This fall in crude oil prices during a time of relative prosperity became the justification for yet another massive transfer of money. This time the OPEC cartel again restricted production enough to cause an artificial shortage that tripled the price of crude oil by reducing production. Even the non-OPEC oil producers jumped on the bandwagon this time. Government taxes fixed as a percentage of crude also rose.

The second transfer was well timed, for it coincided with the roaring nineties (1990-2000) in the west, where a raging stock market bubble obscured any shock to the west and the burgeoning economies of Asia. The consumer by this time was already accustomed to ever-higher or fluctuating prices of gasoline but moreover his pockets were flush with earnings from a raging stock market bubble. The poorer nations of the world suffered greatly, although OPEC compensated them by transferring foreign aid payments.

It is worth noting here that the dictators, monarchs, or military strongmen, who dominate the governments of the OPEC cartel, held true to their Atlantean heritage and pocketed untold trillions without a glitch and with a remarkable acquiescence of most of the world's governments.

## The Looting of the People's Life Savings

Much of the wealth that had accumulated in the west during the postwar years became "lodged" in the personal savings and tax deferred retirement accounts of an aging baby-boomer generation. Huge pension funds, government retirement accounts, corporate retirement accounts, social security, personal savings accounts, and real estate investments accumulated trillions for a generation that was preparing for a comfortable retirement. In addition, the parents of these baby-boomers passed on substantial inheritances to their children.

To get their hands on this money, the agents of The Dark Forces devised a strategy to trick individuals into investing these trillions in the world's stock markets. The money has already disappeared in a proverbial black hole so that by the time the general public awakens, more than thirty trillion dollars will have been transferred to points unknown in The Great Ponzi Scheme of the Nineties-- the largest transfer of wealth in the history of mankind.

## The Great Ponzi Scheme of the 1990s

Innovators of the 1990s brought us the Internet and the personal computer, two instruments that are destined to play a major role in the coming Age of Aquarius. To bring these two inventions to earthly embodiments, the Brotherhood impressed several "geniuses" who in turn created small, innovative companies that developed proprietary software and hardware. Within a few years, these companies had developed such "user friendly" software and hardware that millions in the world could be connected to each other via the Internet. Alongside these revolutionary developments of the incoming Aquarian Age a major sideshow took place that resulted in the largest transfer of wealth and cash in the history of mankind.

**Investment Banks**

Investment bankers around the world seized upon these two innovations and created ancillary companies that would exploit anything tangential to these two inventions. They created the dot.com companies out of virtually nothing, staffed them with young, inexperienced and incompetent personnel, then "took them public." They offered these dot.com company stocks to the public promising exponential returns to the investor.

**Stock Brokerage Firms**

Stock salesmen from their associate stock brokerage firms renamed "Financial Advisors" peddled shares of these new companies to private investors on the international stock markets in the major financial capitals of New York, Hong Kong, London, Frankfurt, Paris, and Taipei. They touted these untried companies as the coming New Age, the New Paradigm, and promised investors such high yields that they would become instant millionaires and retire early with a comfortable income. But the reluctant first-time investor remained hesitant, while the more tried and experienced jumped into the market. The real targets, however, were the reluctant ones who had salted away billions.

## Mutual Funds: Unregulated Groups to Entice the Reluctant

Mutual Funds have been around for several decades. The concept is fairly simple: to pool the money of uninitiated and inexperienced investors and place it with an expert manager. The manager would invest the group's money and the group would divide the profits among themselves after paying the manager a fee.

In the 1990s, thousands of these funds sprung up out of nowhere. Totally *unregulated*, they are under no government authority and thus make up their own rules. Anyone can form a fund without regulation and much mischief has been uncovered.

The funds were sold to the public as the safest way to invest in a very complex roaring stock market. Some funds sold their services under the guise of retirement planning and financial planning. Their brochures bulged with twisted, convoluted legal language that gave them the semblance of legitimacy. Most of all, they touted themselves as experts in "portfolio management" and promised the public handsome returns on their investments for a prosperous retirement. The strategy worked, for they were able to draw in billions, as neighbors and friends emptied their savings and retirement accounts to take part in a financial orgy in the stock market.

Blinded by the prospect of high returns, unsophisticated investors never questioned the fact that these were unregulated funds. By doing so, they gave up complete control of their money to the mutual fund manager, who had no obligation under any law to report to investors what he was doing with their money. In fact, fund managers need not report to anyone, so the investor does not know how much he is really gaining or losing or with whom he is dealing. Curiously, the mutual funds fall into a very gray area of legitimacy, somewhat like the tax revenue agencies, yet they managed to dupe the public into giving them trillions of dollars to manage. How these mutual funds managed to multiply and flourish for a few years, without any apparent government regulations to govern them, will be the subject of future revelations of the power of The Dark Forces working within national governments and banks.

This trio—the investment banks, stock brokerage firms, and the mutual funds—formed the instruments that drew trillions of dollars of hard-earned savings people had tucked away for the future. In addition, they controlled certain finance media consisting of daily 24-hour financial channels and newspapers that provided a sort of cheerleader corps on the sidelines that would whip up a frenzy that would send hordes of people to pour their life savings into equities.

The trio worked in this way: Investment bankers created thousands of unviable companies and hawked them to the general public and the mutual funds. Duped investors poured their money into mutual funds, the mutual funds bought stocks in these companies that had neither products, business experience, nor any track record of profitability.

In order to enable the mutual funds to give initial high returns to their initial investors and thus attract even more into the market, they colluded with the investment banks in a classic Ponzi Scheme.

They introduced shares of new Internet companies with much media fanfare, and by previous arrangement, the mutual funds would buy huge lots of these stocks at a

## Pillaging the Private Sector 81

low price. The effect was to drive the price of the stock higher. By previous agreement, another mutual fund would then bid a higher price for these shares, then still another would buy it for an even higher price and so forth. As the media reported the meteoric rise of a particular company's stock, millions of private investors sought to get in on the action and jumped into the market paying highly inflated prices for these worthless shares, as much as several hundred times their fair value. The smart mutual funds that had already bid the price upward, gladly sold these overpriced stock to the private investors. As share prices soared, more investors poured money into the stock market and mutual funds. The more people saw prices go up, the more they emptied their savings and retirement accounts into the mutual funds.

  After a certain critical mass had been accumulated, the floodgates had opened. Friends and neighbors bragged about the huge returns they were receiving from the mutual funds. They would retire early on a handsome income. The reluctant investor soon cracked open his safe retirement savings and handed it to the mutual funds. If people did not have enough cash to buy stocks, they borrowed it. So much money flooded the market that the mutual funds, investment bankers, and brokerage firms could not produce enough dot.com wonders to fill the demand. Worthless stocks commanded astronomical prices.

  To make use of the flood of savings funds hitting the market, the trio then began speculating on the traditional manufacturing sectors and the so-called blue chip stocks, doing exactly the same thing, artificially bidding prices of stock up, and then unloading them on the greedy latecomers. While the public focused on the hype in the dot.com boom, the telecom, energy, finance, entertainment, public relations, banking, and pharmaceutical sectors were busy inventing ways to grab more of the peoples' retirement savings.

Paper millionaires holding highly inflated stocks sprung up overnight, and the financial capitals rejoiced that a new era of prosperity fueled by the New Economy had arrived. Individual investors loaded with paper profits leveraged their share holdings and bought more shares at the peak of the market hoping it was going to go even higher. On the sidelines, brokerage analysts on the financial television networks cheered the investors on to buy more, promising ever-higher returns and tripling of the stock indices. Prosperity for all, they declared. New York, London, Taipei, Hong Kong etc., boomed.

Brand name designer shops sprouted out of nowhere. Trendy cafes, restaurants, discos, exclusive hotels, luxury cruises, and berthed airliners catered to this new boom-time class of paper millionaires. Finally, the New Age, the new economy, a new economic system had arrived. It would toss out tired old theories of supply and demand and profit and loss to bring in prosperity for all.

Then came March 2000. The great dragon was slain in the astral dimension, and the earth moved into accelerated evolution mode. The flow of new investors into the market began to slow, and the latecomers who had already bought inflated stocks started to panic. "No one wanted to buy these stocks at such a high price!" They began to unload them at any price in a panic sale, and thus the first leg of the stock market crash began. Stock markets around the world plunged and a general panic ensued.

But no market goes straight down, for like a dying beast, it flails about struggling to resuscitate itself until the final moment it succumbs. The stock markets rallied, then plunged, all the time ratcheting lower and lower: rally, crash, rally again, then crash to lower levels in a death process that will hit bottom perhaps in five years. Yet with each rally, the stockbrokers and the media cheer their clients to rush back into the market only to lose more money.

Such will be the fate of the huge stock market bubble of the 1990s. Millions of private investors and the mutual funds now bemoan the huge losses they suffered as the sell-off wiped out their retirement accounts. Yet no one asks the crucial question: **where did the trillions go?**

## The Myth of Stock Market Losses

Money is a condition found only on our planet. It is a form of energy that is represented in coins, bills, credit cards, and automatic wire transfers. Money, like energy, is never lost, unless you are insane enough to deliberately set fire to the bills. Money just changes hands. During the days of the gold standard, you could even melt down a gold coin, and it would still retain its value. In other words, money is indestructible. It just goes from hand to hand.

You "lose" money when someone robs or swindles you of it. If you are the loser, there is a winner. It's quite simple because money is a manifestation of indestructible cosmic energy. So, who are the winners in this great money orgy of the 1990s?

### 1. Corporate Thieves

Today, newspapers quietly mention the vast sums that corporate officers misspent to create a system of underwater broadband cables stretching around the world that no one can use, high tech skyscrapers, office complexes and shopping centers, satellites, private jets, mansions, country clubs, and the like. Company executives looted their firms with grossly inflated salaries, redeemed stock options profiting from "insider information," dumped worthless stocks for the public to buy, made illegal loans to themselves, and transferred huge sums to offshore corporations, and plotted with highly paid auditors to fudge the accounts and dupe the public.

By design, government regulators reacted, rather than anticipated the great crimes of the corporate world, and thus were too late to stop any of the malfeasance. Today, they must try to reconstruct certain cases but the full extent of corporate malfeasance will never be known, for many corporate officers have already absconded with their booty leaving their companies bankrupt shells in the hands of debtors. Many have disappeared to offshore havens which were set up years before in order to protect finance fugitives from prosecution. Many will change their names, obtain new passports and identities, and resume their activities.

Too much money flowed into corporate hands, and the temptation became irresistible: corporate boards of directors, chief executive officers, and chief financial officers colluded with their accounting auditors to abscond with billions by transferring them overseas to dummy offshore companies covering these thefts with inflated stocks and derivatives.

Many innocent investors have realized considerable losses, but they also do not realize that these losses represent massive gains for these forces. Investment banks set up these companies, put their own people at the helm, created the media hype about their future, cheered investors to buy stock in the company,

## Pillaging the Private Sector

manipulated the price of these stocks on the stock market until the company had on their accounting books an artificially high valuation. They then pillaged real assets of the companies. When the stock value crashed, all that was left was a bankrupt shell.

These blatant crimes against the investor should have been enough to close down the stock markets forever, but they continue to trick those who are trying to recover their losses into investing even more. Stockholders are now fighting back, lawsuits abound against accounting and brokerage firms, corporate executives, and the people who were supposed to protect the public, the auditors. Everyone is in a fury, and rightfully so. But, unfortunately, we wish to point out again, that this was just a carefully planned and orchestrated sideshow to divert your attention from the real crime being carried out.

Although in collusion with The Dark Forces, most of the corporate leadership are but front men—the attractive, seemingly competent ones placed in key positions to draw in investors' money with their charm and media exposure. Many of the corporate elite in the investment banking and stock brokerage firms industries are young, impressionable souls, naive in that they are dazzled by the money making prospects those of The Dark Forces' fostered. By appealing to their greed and need for media notoriety, they in essence serve as fall guys of a scheme so much more insidious and complex than the public can imagine, for the ones pushing the buttons and manipulating the markets are never seen. The fall guys got caught with their hands in the till, while others were cunning enough to escape scrutiny and prosecution.

The public will continue to vent their wrath through the courts and media, but one thing is certain, the public will never get its money back. While the public's attention is tied up in the plodding prosecution of corporate thieves, trillions more will disappear. Again, where did the money really go?

## 2. Corporate Debt

The private investor who bought equity shares or securities essentially exchanged his money for a piece of paper called a corporate stock certificate. He thought he bought a piece of a company and thus would share in the profits (or losses) of that company. These corporations spent most of the capital from these stock sales on wild schemes until nothing was left. To survive, they pledged the corporation's assets in order to borrow huge sums of money that would keep them afloat.

The equity share that the investor thought he bought became worthless without his knowledge when the corporation pledged the company assets to borrow money. Unsophisticated investors continued to purchase the corporation's worthless shares on the stock market at inflated prices as the media painted a rosy picture of the corporation's future. The inflated share values became the sole worth of the company. As long as the raging stock market kept going, this corporate debt would not be exposed.

Finally, the stock market crash exposed more and more corporations to be but empty shells, heavily in debt, and on the brink of bankruptcy. What happened to the cash these corporations borrowed on the corporation's assets? It disappeared into the derivatives' black hole.

### 3. Derivatives: The Black Hole

Many remember the young rogue trader in Singapore who lost a fortune on derivatives and brought about the downfall of one of England's most venerable banks. The major world stock exchanges invented derivatives to draw more cash into the marketplace. With a derivative, the speculator buys the right to place a bet on the direction of a given market. For example, an investor will purchase a gold futures contract on the hope that gold prices will either go up or go down. We emphasize that the investor can make money if a given market goes up or down, not only up. If he bets the market will drop, and the market indeed drops, he wins and vice versa. If the markets do not go his way, he loses his money.

Investing in derivatives is simply a bet, a form of gambling, although it is cloaked as a legitimate form of investment. It is highly speculative and risky. In addition to these public derivative offerings, there is also a private derivatives market, which we know exists, but little is known about its parameters. What is important to remember is that in these so-called derivative markets, for every winner there is a loser. This is the key to elucidating where all the money is going.

It is a treacherous game because the markets are manipulated. So powerful are The Dark Forces that they can cause prices of commodity futures to go in any direction they want. For example, they will manipulate the price of gold by buying thousands of futures contracts to "go long." This very act will cause the gold price to go up. They spread the word through the media that gold prices are soaring and will reach a certain high price at the end of the year. An upward trend is thus established.

Hearing the rumors, thousands of investors, corporations, banks, and mutual funds rush in to buy gold futures contracts betting that the price of gold will be at a certain level by the end of the year. The rush into the market itself has a momentary self-fulfilling prophecy, for it causes the price of gold to mount even higher. When the price reaches high enough levels for a healthy profit, these forces jump out and realize huge profits.

If the gold market continues up a little more, then these forces jump back in, "sell into" or "short" the gold market, or bet that gold prices will start to fall. This creates a small panic and people start selling. As the price of gold plunges, these forces bag another huge amount in profits.

Because of their financial power, The Dark Forces can determine in which direction they want the market to go. In the beginning they entice investors, corporations, pension funds, and banks to invest "allowing" them a fine return on their money. This encourages them to invest even greater sums in derivatives. Again, they realize some handsome profits. Confident after these gains, they invest an even greater percentage of their portfolio in derivatives. With the derivatives market bulging with expectation that a given market will move one way, The Dark Forces step in and force the markets in the opposite direction. These investors lose everything and The Dark Forces haul away the massive sums of cash.

This is one of the principal ways trillions in cash have been drained from the world's corporations and banks until it reaches its final destination in the coffers of The Dark Forces. For all of the corporate or individual losers, there were winners. And the winners reaped trillions.

### 4. Mergers and Acquisitions

At the height of the great stock market bubble there was a surge of mergers and acquisitions among the new paradigm companies. Holding companies bought and sold companies like commodities. Riding on the inflated values of a company's stock, the prices companies paid for their acquisition were at the top of the market, defying all business sense of buying low and selling high. If you took away the company's stock values, there would be virtually nothing left in terms of hard assets or a business model.

When company A wanted to buy Company B, it not only bought Company B's inflated stocks, but it also had to pay an extra premium of goodwill. Some companies paid billions in goodwill, which is to say they bought billions of dollars of air. Media fanfare and sideline cheering accompanied each of these deals to entice more investors to buy the stock of the newly created merger and keep the values high.

Untold billions changed hands during this frenzy of mergers and acquisitions and those who walked away with their pockets full were the same ones who had manipulated the market to such heights. This seemingly endless and lucrative game ended as the stock markets began to plunge, but it would be safe to speculate that the stock market losses experienced by innocent, yet greedy investors, are safely tucked away in the banks of Switzerland.

### 5. The Mutual Funds: The Ultimate Black Hole

We pointed out above the unregulated nature of the mutual funds. They can do anything with your money and you have absolutely no recourse. There are no third party audits and their annual financial reports to the investors are fine works of fiction. All we can say is what happens in the secret back rooms of the mutual fund headquarters is detrimental to mankind. The fact remains that like the tax revenue services, they answer to no authority. They can do what they want, and there is no one to check or verify their actions. Managers say losses in the general equities markets are causing these losses, but are they? How can the public know since these funds are not required to report their holdings, gains or losses?

The mutual fund phenomenon also distorts the so-called market forces in the stock markets where free exchange of equities is touted. Instead of millions of small investors in the market exchanges, a few thousand mutual fund managers control trillions of dollars of equities and are thus able to manipulate the rise and fall of certain stocks. Thus, they control the rise or fall of the stock market indices with their huge holdings of corporate stocks. Through their huge blocks of stocks they hold in companies, they also exert influence on the decisions in the boardrooms of these companies.

In the meantime, mutual fund investors watch their investments diminish, month by month. The smart ones have already withdrawn what's left of their capital, while the hopefuls hang on as these "losses" gradually fritter away their principal. By the time the public wakes up to this massive deception, mutual funds will have tumbled like all of the other top-heavy organizations. Part of the trillions that investors "lost" will be traced to the dark underworld of transactions that the mutual funds engaged in without outside verification or accountability in the derivatives markets.

These sinister inventions of The Dark Forces form the ultimate black hole, the funnel into the banks in

Switzerland. Yet as the markets gradually collapse over the next few years, these once towers of finance will wither away.

## The End is Nigh

Many who pulled their money out of the stock market early enough, and saved what was left of their capital, rushed to invest these funds in real estate, but again this mad rush created yet another bubble of inflated real estate. Finance companies, mortgage brokers, and banks readily accorded mortgage loans to these buyers. Once they obtained the signature of the borrower on the loan papers, they sold the mortgages to secondary mortgage corporations. In order to purchase these mortgages, the latter, in turn, borrow the money by issuing debt securities and notes, much like the government does to pay for the national debt, to the powerful financiers of The Dark Forces.

In essence, through this convoluted maze of borrowing, the agents of The Dark Forces own indirectly most properties purchased with a mortgage. In other words, if you do not own the real estate 100 percent, the mortgage holder, which is itself indebted to The Dark Forces, is the true owner.

As the world economy deflates, more and more people will lose their jobs, the consequence being, they will not have the money to make payments on their mortgages. They will default on their house payments and be thrown out into the streets and these sinister secondary mortgage corporations will take possession of the property.

When mortgage defaults reach a critical mass, the secondary mortgage corporations will collapse leaving a wasteland of properties. This will spell the end to the financial grip The Dark Forces hold on the world.

## The Other World

In the sections above, we learned how The Dark Forces concentrated their efforts on the wealthy countries of the world during the last years of Twentieth Century. They have been able to drain the affluent populations of the world of their money through cleverly devised schemes that exploited the free market system of the West. But this does not mean that they have ignored the rest of the world.

The majority of people on this earth can barely scratch out a living, much less, have extra money to speculate on the stock market. The impoverished masses of the world are divided among many sovereign nation-states. We mention the word "sovereign," for under this rubric much can be accomplished within the borders of impoverished sovereign states, away from international public scrutiny.

Unable to squeeze any significant tax revenue from poverty-ridden people, except at gunpoint, and moreover, fearful of pushing the impoverished so far that they will revolt out of desperation, The Dark Forces have used more feudal means to control money.

There is a certain favored class that invariably rises out of impoverished situations. It is one intimately connected to those who hold power within the government bureaucracy. The intimate interchanges between the government and this favored class usually involves the exploitation of the country's major natural resources, like mineral mines, plantations, drugs, cement or crude oil. The favored class pays government officials handsomely for certain concessions and applies or obtains the know-how and capital to exploit the resources. Handsome amounts from these concessions pass between these two parties and invariably flow out of the country into foreign banks in Switzerland or other offshore havens.

Government officials enrich themselves and live in the country's finest mansions. The favored class enjoys the life of the jet setter. They often live in fenced-in or walled communities surrounded by tight security usually on a plateau or higher ground overlooking the city capital. Many flaunt their wealth before the impoverished masses, for often they are blind to the misery around them. Often, the families of the favored class intermarry with those of other countries so that there is a social and business network linking them together.

They own private jets that wing them to the major capitals of the world where they wine, dine, and shop in the finest boutiques with their domestics and bodyguards in tow. On every trip they carry massive amounts of cash, to deposit in bank accounts in Switzerland or other offshore havens.

The Dark Forces exploit what they can, using the less sophisticated methods of their Atlantean roots. The impoverished populations provide the cheap labor to exploit these concessions. In some countries, the governments or these large concessions give out food rations that limit a person's intake of food to what is prescribed on the ration card. This is one of the means by which the forces can control the masses, for what hungry person would revolt against the authority that controls his food supply?

Although the exploitation of the impoverished continues in a most feudalistic manner, they are minor players compared to the lucrative schemes of the equities and financial markets in the more advanced economies. What is noteworthy here is that The Dark Forces are in every corner of the world weaving their financial grip on humanity. No matter how poverty-stricken the people are, they never stop from extracting more, even when the countries' people are on the brink of starvation. Fortunately, some good and advanced souls have elected to incarnate into these favored classes and do battle with their practices. All should come to a head in the Armageddon and the grip these dictators and entourages have on humanity will be a thing of the past.

## The Slow Agonizing Death of the Dragon

When the new millennium arrived, the Great Cosmic Beings who oversee earth said, "Enough!" They stepped on the accelerator and earth spun into high speed acceleration, one that would drive The Dark Forces insane and finally weed them off the earth plane.

The effect on the stock markets was almost immediate. The party ended in March 2000, when the first panic selling began. The more intelligent investors suspected that such a party could not last forever and perhaps, just perhaps, they were holding worthless inflated paper. They got out right away. The more unsophisticated and hopeful investor, the one following his greedy instincts rather than reason, stayed in the market hoping for the good times to come back. But the stock markets around the world continued their downward slide, wiping out the unviable dot.com businesses and sending even the bluest of the blue chip corporations to the brink of bankruptcy. Millions of investors, who remained in the market at the urging and advice of their stockbrokers and advisors, lost trillions of dollars. Those who hang on with the slightest thread of hope that the markets will recover will lose even more.

The managers of the world's stock exchanges today continue to convince investors the plunge is only a short-term correction. "Just stay in there for the long-term. Weather the downturn and in a few years everything will be fine," chants the media. Yet the economies of the world have continued down the slippery slope. Trillions more are to be lost as the top-heavy towers of the world of finance plunge into the abyss.

But like derivatives, the markets are structured so that the knowing manipulators can win on the upswing as well as the downswing. The forces that reaped the profits while the markets went up, will also reap much when they go down. The big difference this time is that the institutions and instruments used to steal and amass the wealth will be weakened on each downturn until they are destroyed, never to be resurrected. It is the great dragon gasping his last breaths of air before its ultimate demise.

The Dark Forces know their days are numbered and in desperation they will try to take everything and everyone down with them. They will try to stave off the plunge in the stock market, which began in 2000, and spread an illusion of a genuine economic recovery. By doing this, they will draw back skeptical investors, only to run off with their money when the fundamentals of the markets take over again and force the markets down again. How many times they can pull this trick on the public will depend on how gullible it is, but gradually over the next few years, this process will die out and the stock markets will be silenced.

## The Price of Consent

The massive transfer of wealth from millions of retirement and savings accounts into the coffers of The Dark Forces could only have happened with the consent of the good and innocent souls of mankind. When people have finally awakened to what has happened, they will turn against all these institutions that have stolen, rather than served them. They will storm the mutual funds, outlaw the derivatives market, and even outlaw the stock exchanges. What no one will be able to deny is that The Dark Forces merely set the trap, and the unthinking, weak souls, motivated by greed or the dreams painted by the agents of The Dark Forces, willingly walked into it.

As these towers of financial systems and markets gradually crumble and are drained of their money, The Dark Forces will turn to their other specialty—warmongering—in a desperate attempt to maintain their grip on mankind.

# CHAPTER 6
## Masters of War
*"Truth is the first victim of war."*

The threat of terrorism preys on the minds of humanity today. It would be so much easier to accept the scenario of events leading up to the attack of September 11, as presented in the mass media. Using a bit of logic we should question the accepted scenario of what happened. How is it that the greatest military country in the world could have been so lax in its security measures to allow some motley rogue force from the caves of Afghanistan to suddenly come over and very successfully, within a matter of an hour or so, attack the two most famous financial buildings in New York City and then go on to attack the Pentagon itself--and with no retaliation whatever?

Could it be possible that these events could be nothing more than part of an orchestrated scenario to further the ends of The Dark Forces? Is it possible that the struggle against terrorism is but a game being played on a chessboard, rather than the crusade it is made out to be? Could acts of terrorism in reality be well-planned events designed to direct public opinion to war?

In the case of the attack on the New York World Trade Center on September 11, 2001, it was choreographed very beautifully before live news broadcasts throughout the world. It all went off like clockwork, because that's precisely what it was, not a coincidence, but a well-choreographed scenario.

Is it not odd that so few question these events and those who do are branded as fools? From where we sit, we can affirm that this was not the work of terrorists out of Afghanistan. This was not the work of some cult group called the Taliban. This was the work of The Dark Forces we have referenced above. It is part of a greater plan to create world crisis and prepare everyone for a state of war.

The World Trade Center attack and the way it has led up to the War with Iraq is quite similar to events leading up to the War in Vietnam, except in the case of the latter, it was the threat of Communism instead of terrorism. Again, using a bit of logic, was this little tiny country in Southeast Asia really a threat to the U.S.? Any intelligent person could see that Vietnam posed no direct threat to the security of the U.S., yet after getting rid of their principal obstacle, President Kennedy, and engineering the Gulf of Tonkin incident, The Dark Forces were able to get Washington, D.C. to deploy thousands upon thousands of young men to lose their lives, lose their minds, and lose their limbs. For what?

What was really being defended? What was the threat? Communism? But after the long tragic war, the Communists did indeed take over Vietnam, which posed no threat to the U.S. Any thinking individual would have known in the early sixties that there was no threat at all, any more than there is any threat to you right now from any of the so-called terrorists groups you might find on this planet.

## Wars—Planned and Orchestrated Events

You might ask, for what purpose do The Dark Forces create war? Money is the most obvious answer. Wars are not spur-of-the-moment events: They are planned events, carefully laid out, and plotted years in advance. The war in Iraq has taken at least ten years to plan. Planes, missiles, ships, satellites, and all the war materiel take years to design and build. This is often justified under "being prepared" for defense purposes. Is it not strange that the media broadcasts the step-by-step mobilization of war these days? Does this war coverage not look like a vast show for the public to view from their television sets?

Could the attack on the World Trade Center be viewed as merely one scene in the unfoldment of a complex plan to create a public mind set for war? There is nothing like modern warfare, now so dependent on high technology and material, to keep the factories humming and the bank accounts full. So as they did in previous incarnations, The Dark Forces continue to plot, plan, and execute wars for gain.

Wars and armed conflict have yet another insidious goal: they divert people's attention away from their normal lives so that laws or decrees can be passed to strip away whatever rights they might have had. And when the conflict is over, people suddenly realize that an even more repressive regime has taken over. We need only look at the aftermath of World War II, when half the world—Soviet Union, Eastern Europe, Central Asia, China, North Korea and Southeast Asia-- came under repressive, dictatorial regimes. Even now, the so-called security measures at the airports and borders, are all designed to get people used to being searched, to being submissive, to not question, to giving up their sense of freedom, and to preventing them from coming and going at will. These are the same tired and tedious reinventions of past practices of repression.

Further bills will be introduced into legislatures and communities to suppress the private ownership of firearms, which is guaranteed in the American Constitution as every man's right. We are not diehard firearm advocates but wish to remind you that the original intent of this provision was this: The founding fathers of the American Constitution wanted to make sure that citizens could defend their right to be governed by the people and for the people, if and when, the insane who claim to govern them, turn against them.

## War at All Costs

When a war has been meticulously planned, its execution will proceed at all cost, and The Dark Forces will mow down anyone or thing that gets in their way. Governments, the main perpetrator of wars, will boldly and baldly lie to their citizens about the human and material costs of wars and their consequences. What will seem like the enemy is in reality also part of the game. They will engage the full force of the media to mercilessly chant their justifications and viewpoint of the war until it has been drummed into every citizen's mind. This sounds brutal and bestial at best, but very much in line with their low level of evolutionary development.

In the Oliver Stone production of the movie *JFK*, the credits should have read, "Directed by J.F.K himself," for indeed it was. That the spirit once known as President

J.F. Kennedy had lobbied the authorities of the Brotherhood for sometime to get the true story of his assassination told to the public. And indeed, he got his wish. Give or take a few facts, the movie presented the true scenario of what unfolded. It exposed the fallacious theory of the magic bullet, the one that felled the President, then zigzagged, turned around and hit the Governor of Texas. In a recent television interview with the former Texas Governor and his wife, they also confirmed multi-shots hit them. Yet despite their testimony, the government's official report on the assassination of the President has never been changed.

Most shockingly, Mr. Oswald didn't fire a shot at all, yet he is the one whom history records as the assassin of John F. Kennedy. In fact, he served as the fall guy, the scapegoat of a much deeper plot. The movie also pointed out that within 24 hours, Mr. Oswald's whole biography was splashed all over the world just as if it had been prepared. How quick!

In truth, President Kennedy was assassinated simply because he refused to give his consent to carry out a war in Vietnam. We point out this sad event to show the reader how belligerent The Dark Forces can be, for they wanted to prove that even if the President of the United States were to oppose their plans for war, he would be eliminated. "We can blow the head off of your President at high noon, in front of all of you, can't we?"

The assassination also highlights how The Dark Forces can pressure many leaders of countries throughout the world to adhere to their agenda. It did not take President Kennedy's successor long to sign the orders to send five hundred thousand troops into war.

Once the War in Vietnam was well on its way, The Dark Forces unleashed their power to sabotage the Vietnam peace movement. Many newspaper reporters of the day agree that peace advocate and singer, Miss Janis Joplin, had been murdered. She did not die of a self-inflicted heroin overdose, any more than Mr. Jimmy Hendrix did that same year. It was common knowledge they all indulged in drugs, but using a bit of logic, most people who indulge in those things, like good chemists, know what it takes to get high. They are not likely to take huge amounts of the drug all of a sudden. It's a matter of public record that the L.A. County coroner reported in his autopsy that Miss Joplin's body contained an amount of heroin that was forty or fifty times more potent than anything you would ever find on the street. Could it be that someone fed her this high dose? We are sorry to say this is so.

Why would The Dark Forces focus on these musicians? One year before, in 1969, the Woodstock Peace Concert took place and much to the amazement of the authorities, young people from all over the U.S. came together without any incident. There were no deaths, no murders, no violence–everyone actually got along quite peacefully. When The Dark Forces realized that this event could be reproduced over and over again, they immediately targeted their leaders and within a short year, in 1970, all of them were dead. What a coincidence!

Efforts to thwart their warmongering often meet with tragedy, for The Dark Forces are always on the alert for any people or forces that successfully promote unity or cause people to work together. Their methods have not changed since the days of Mr. Adolph Hitler whose motto was to "Divide and conquer. Divide and conquer." They deliberately perpetrate and inflame racial tensions, ethnic conflicts, and any differences in order to keep people focused on how much they hate each other and how this country differs from another, and why this race is superior to another. UNITY is their enemy. Anyone or anything that promotes similarities over differences will be their enemy. Today these same methods apply. The Dark Forces have planned puppets of hatred like Osama Bin Laden. He is put before the eyes for the world to promote hatred and to be hated, in this case, along religious lines.

Warmongering is thus their ultimate activity, the culmination of years of plotting and planning of The Dark Forces, who with their considerable financial power, can goad nations into warring with each in order to make even more money. This tedious cycle has been repeated over and over during the centuries it took to build our present civilization. In the process, they tighten the noose around the sheep that follow, stripping them even more of their freedoms and rights.

Use your imagination as to how those forces holding the national debts of key nations in the world can exert power and influence on the leaders of indebted countries. If they were to call in the debt of the U.S. alone, it would bring that great country to its knees. So when certain countries wage war in the name of whatever ideal they might cite at that moment, we must remember that they are responding to forces way beyond their own borders.

Thus when we analyze the War in Iraq, we can conclude that both sides are essentially on the same side, the side of darkness. Again, we emphasize that The Dark Forces have no nationality. They merely exploit division and conflict in the world in order to create wars. And if a potential combatant nation is reluctant to conduct war, these forces will create the conditions and justifications so that the nation will want to go to war!

Every war is a battle between light and darkness. The forces of darkness manipulate the combatants into war using whatever financial leverage and sophistry to egg them on. These "trumped up" wars succeed if we do not take the right stance, for by cosmic law, we give our approbation if we remain silent and do not say, "No, enough!" Each and every one of us being directly connected to God, can stand on the side of Light and beam upon the warring parties Love and Light. This is the true stance to take.

As we beam Divine Light and Love on the two warring parties, the world will observe how their war plans will go awry, missiles will miss their intended mark, grenades and mines will lie dead, and "friendly fire" incidents will increase. The workers in the war ministries will question daily what they are doing, and the death of each innocent being will, repulse his killer. The warring leaders themselves will be jolted into the realization that there will never be a victor out of all the misery and hardship they have caused, and as we continue to beam forth Light and Love, the guns will gradually fall silent. There is always an end to war.

## The Ultimate Triumph of Light

And so we have reached these times so long ago predicted in the holy scriptures of many of the world's religions. It is the end of a cycle when earth has decided it will no longer put up with this situation. It is also a time when The Dark Forces will muster the last of its dark power to forge one last stand, yet another world war, the Third World War in the years to come. But this time, the Masters of the Great Brotherhood of Light will take up this ultimate challenge and rid the earth of The Dark Forces, once and for all. It is the time when the Great and Holy Master Sanctus Germanus will lead the forces of Light in a magnificent turn about and when it does, soul liberation will at last return to earth. It is a war of sorts between them and He, and all souls will form to the right or the left of that realization. This is the nature of the Armageddon today.

## A note on disease and pestilence

During the Armageddon we can expect The Dark Forces to resort to other desperate attempts to regain their footing on the world stage. They will attempt to disseminate fear in the minds of everyone, so that the individual will seek the protection of government.

During their last days, one disease after another will be broadcast over the airwaves, to intimidate and cower humanity. Out of these mysterious, unseen microbes or viruses (computer viruses included) governments and the media will seize the opportunity to create mass fear and hysteria in order to cower humanity into submitting to government control that promises to protect them. Frightened people cannot exercise their liberties and freedoms or fight back. They become submissive, an ideal condition as far as The Dark Forces are concerned.

In return for this protection, governments will invade the last bastion of individual privacy—the human body itself. Individuals will be subjected to tests and probes of their vital parts and quarantined. All in preparation for getting people used to being restrained.

It is no accident that the origins of these diseases are always exotic places, for the unknown always causes more fear. We hear about the Asian Flu, the West Nile Virus, Ebola, the Hong Kong flu, and the like which strike fear of certain races purported to be the originators of the disease. Divide and conquer has been the motto of these Atlantean souls for millennia.

# CHAPTER 7
## The Armageddon: A Cosmic Filtering Process

Many who hear the word *Armageddon* conger up pictures of the whole world blowing up in some kind of world conflict and becoming scattered pieces in an asteroid belt. Many born-again Christians believe that they will be lifted off the earth in a great rapture, leaving the sinners to battle it out until earth's ultimate demise. Many New Age hopefuls have already proclaimed the arrival of the Age of Aquarius, even as we wallow in starvation, wars, and materialism. That earth's problems should be so easily resolved and with such finality could only be the result of a profound misunderstanding of the whole process of human evolution, for as we noted in Chapter One, our journey of millions of years is far from over.

## The Filtering Process

Our view of the Armageddon differs considerably from the current thought in that we see it more as a filtering process—separating the tares from the wheat, the light from darkness—in every pore, level, and sector of human society, for the true objective of the Armageddon is a general, comprehensive housecleaning designed to rid the earth plane of all negative influences, those of The Dark Forces, so that the conditions necessary for the flowering of a new golden age, the Age of Aquarius, can prevail.

In this filtering process, everyone will be given a chance to play out his or her true self and those who are not suited to remain on the earth plane, by their chosen actions or beliefs, will be shifted to other planets that are more in line with their thinking. The filtering process will touch every being on earth, without exception, for astrological pulls and influences as well as the acceleration in the earth's evolution (see below) will bring out everyone's true colors. And how will you know how to distinguish one from another? "By their fruits, ye shall know them," said the Great and Holy Master Jesus.

The significance of this comprehensive filtering process is this: there will be disturbance on every level of human society until every stone has been turned and the dark characteristics or forces are filtered out. Your nearest and dearest may be affected and turn against you. Brother will turn against brother, father against son, sister against sister and so forth, until the whole population on the earth plane is purified.

## Victory on the Higher Dimensions

The final battle between light and darkness is the project of the Great and Holy Master Sanctus Germanus. This great Master of the Great Brotherhood of Light has taken his place as the Hierarch of the New Age, the Age of Aquarius. He leads the battle. Those souls who are for Him stand on the right, while those who oppose him shall be banished from the earth plane.

On the higher dimensions, the Master St. Germain has already plunged the sword of truth through the heart of the symbolic dragon of evil. As it lies clinging to life, the giant tail of the dying beast periodically whiplashes from side to side, with each whiplash, Wham! It sends shockwaves down to the earth plane. So what we are experiencing are the clean up operations of this great slaughter. Yes, it's messy. Its agents on earth desperately try to reverse their inevitable demise, creating the turmoil and conflict we sense here on earth as they struggle to save themselves. But cosmic law has already determined that their cycle is up—finished—and that the Forces of Light shall prevail in this battle.

The battle has already been won on the higher planes, which is why we can be so sure of the outcome on earth. As painful as it might be, however, the final battles will take place over the next decade.

## Acceleration of Earth's Evolution

Have you not remarked how time flies these days? Days, weeks, months and years seem to streak by. Barely into one month, you awaken to find yourself starting a new month. And so from the point of view of time, you begin to perceive events in life take place at an accelerated pace.

When the clock struck midnight on December 31, 1999, the earth spun into an accelerated mode of evolution. Great Beings concerned with earth decreed this acceleration. Did the planet have any power to resist? Certainly not. The soul of Earth is organic, alive, and also in the process of becoming. Earth and other planetary bodies are but the vehicles, the bodies, of great souls that inhabit them. Each planet has a spirit, a being in the process of evolution that is ensouled in the physical mass. Thus each planet has its nature, its qualities just as you do. So, when Great Cosmic Beings associated with the planet earth determined that it was lagging in its evolution, they simply said, "Move a little faster," and the earth obeyed and sped up.

By cosmic design, the acceleration of the earth also serves as the *agent provocateur* of the events, which we define as the period of the Armageddon. It acts essentially as a catalyst that provokes into action the final battle between Light and Darkness on every level of society. Earth becomes like a bullet train heading for higher enlightenment. The bright light at the end of the tunnel disturbs some. They turn away from it and do not want to go there. So they must get off and find another train more suitable for their state of mind at this time. But those good innocent souls who search only that great objective of liberating their souls so they can blossom forth, joyfully stay on for the high-speed ride, for they know that when they reach that destination of light, they will all have gotten there because they wanted to. And what great joy it is to travel with those with whom you are compatible!

**General Effects of Acceleration**

Acceleration produces a state of insanity on earth, in short, bedlam. A tempest. A gale. It won't be easy for the next few years to come. Those on earth who were barely hanging on will begin to find themselves going a little haywire. The effect of acceleration is like asking a driver who can barely keep his car on the road at 25 miles per hour to suddenly accelerate to 100 miles per hour. He'll lose control and run off the road!

A mother-in-law suddenly turns sour toward her

## Cosmic Filtering Process

lovely daughter-in-law, your son turns inward and becomes excessively involved in the computer, a daughter snaps back at her mother, fathers scrap with their sons and vice versa, your dear spouse suddenly turns cold and uncommunicative, and an old friend no longer wants to see you. You, yourself, might find yourself screaming at a store clerk or furious at another driver cutting in front of you, and wonder afterwards, what got into you.

These general manifestations of insanity are the more benign variety. They touch everyone, for everyone is sort of "edgy." This is due to a slight and temporary disconnection between the conscious mind and the soul due to the speed of things, and the lack of conscious control to realign oneself with the soul in meditation or prayers. These benign signs of the Armageddon are fortunately temporary.

When your nearest and dearest exhibit this temporary insanity or imbalance of the mental body, the first thing you must do is ascertain to what degree that you should be out of striking distance while they are in that state. Consider them hysterical. They can do anything and are unpredictable. You must take care of yourself, but at the same time, you cannot blame them. But you need not play the martyr either and think, "Oh, she'll respond to me!" She or he might just strike back at you or say something that is equally shocking that will cause a permanent schism in your relationship. Yes, at one time perhaps you were on good terms with this person. Then suddenly, he or she begins acting quite rudely to you. What have you done wrong? Nothing?

Know that the situation is temporary, and hope that the relationship will eventually be restored if indeed there was true love and respect in the relationship to begin with. Learn to be good caretakers. If you must leave someone's presence because there is some danger in staying, then move on. Do not waver when you feel that you've done nothing to warrant the treatment. But if you have done something wrong, you'll want to admit it. But when you are insulted, slighted or ignored for no good reason or suddenly someone you thought you were on good terms with treats you like a stranger or worse, it's time to ascertain if the situation is one of temporary insanity. Then get out of the range of fire during that temporary period.

**Malign Manifestations of Acceleration**

Acceleration also affects those harboring more malign forms of criminality. Rashes of crimes break out. A student goes berserk in a high school and mows down his friends with a machine gun in the U.S. Another student does the same thing in Europe. Suddenly, young women are being abducted in various parts of the world. Or serial killers start stalking women in various countries. Or worse, snipers randomly pick off innocent victims from the ends of their rifles. Husbands stalk their estranged wives and shoot their own children. Mothers beat their infant children until they succumb. Wives run down their unfaithful husbands with the family car. This is bedlam but symptomatic of the times we are in.

More heinous crimes come to light such as mass murders, serial killings, ethnic cleansing, mass torture, wars, and the like. Those hidden, lurking criminally inclined individuals suddenly cannot take the pressure any longer of the acceleration. They go berserk, and expose themselves for what they really are. They are one-by-one eliminated from the face of the earth.

Old religious sores will rise to the surface with

# Cosmic Filtering Process 113

Islamic fundamentalists striking out at their old Christian or Hindu enemies. Even different sects within one religion will contradict the other, leading to schisms. Fundamentalist Christians lash out at their black brothers with their white supremacist ideology, while another sect attacks the Jews for their crucifixion of Jesus. All religious differences come to the surface, some resulting in outward conflict, while others resulting in healing. Politicians, public figures or entertainers presenting one face to the world but hiding prejudices or agendas of a less noble nature will suddenly find themselves blurting out their true feelings and exposing their prejudices, evil intentions or their outright stupidity in front of the cameras or in public. World leaders contradict each other, previous international alliances end up splintered by dissent and posturing, friendly nations turn against one another behind the scene. Many fallen leaders wonder how they managed to lose control over their tongues, yet they have exposed themselves. Their former power to block or sabotage programs that benefit mankind or mesmerize the public is fortunately stunted.

Again, these are the signs of the Armageddon, the filtering out process of the bad eggs.

## Process of Macro Economic Dispossession

In March 2000, reacting to the acceleration, the New York stock exchange suddenly plunged after almost a decade of wild speculation. Other markets and bourses around the world followed suit and a worldwide meltdown of these towers of finance continues. The Dark Forces anticipated an eventual plunge of the financial markets but perhaps were taken by surprise at the suddenness of the downturn. Like the dying dragon in the upper dimensions, these stock exchanges struggle to rally, only to be hammered to new lows. Up again then down further, their value ratchets down the slippery slide. Huge unknown forces pump huge sums of money into the market to force the market upward. The innocent investor, thinking the worst is over, rushes back into the market, and these unknown forces sell out to these naive ones and back out. Again the market plunges taking with it more investor cash. It is obvious that The Dark Forces intend to drag everyone down with them as they drain the last cent out of all the cash cows they created.

In a secret hall in the middle of Europe, the powerful leaders behind these benighted individuals plot yet more wars, concentrating at times in the Middle East. These wars, as we mentioned earlier, are but manipulated and orchestrated events. They do not involve one righteous nation fighting against the evil one. Both, one could say, are on the same side, for it is but a game. But during these times, these games will run amuck as the light from the Brotherhood is directed toward these events.

Wars are coordinated with the collapse of the stock markets where The Dark Forces take massive short positions to bleed as much money as possible from the markets as they plunge. A war victory produces a false sense of well-being on the side of the victor and the euphoria causes the markets to rejoice and soar upward. On the upward swing, more innocent investors pour their last bits of cash into the equities market hoping to recover their losses from the previous downturn. The-forces-that-be will again sell (short sell) their inflated equities to these innocent investors and mutual funds in order to reap more money as the stock markets again plunge. The investors, never learning and always tricked, will again be left holding the bag of worthless stocks.

With each plunge, companies which relied upon their stocks to give worth to their balance sheets will be hammered and will eventually go bankrupt. The stock exchanges themselves will shrink as more and more investors get slaughtered. The kingpins of the world of brokerage will one by one close their doors and the investment bank will wither away for lack of new business. Banks will fail, one after another, as their arrogance gives way to revelations of activities that will be their own undoing. The unregulated mutual funds will close their doors and their irate investors will storm their empty offices only to find that someone has walked off with trillions of dollars of their life savings.

As the dragon dies in the upper spheres, these top-heavy towers of finance that so controlled the world's financial system are being slain. Another five or so years they will be lowered into the pits from whence they came.

But those who planned and perpetrated these institutions for as long as they could, will end up taking trillions from the people and storing them in the caves of iniquity.

With the capital markets virtually annihilated, corporations large and small will begin to deflate. So heavily in debt are these corporations from their speculations in the stock markets and derivatives, that their debt holder, primarily banks, will be forced to seize their assets. On and on, the deflationary spiral will gradually wipe out business after business leaving only those which were wise enough to resist getting into debt or those businesses that cater to the barest survival services.

As businesses close their doors, millions will lose their jobs and then their homes and possessions. Prices as a consequence will deflate, and deflation will cause even more businesses to close down. Then the banks will be so overwhelmed by "nonperforming debt" that they themselves will sink. Then, The Dark Forces plan to step in for the kill and seize the banks and lenders with their collateral assets.

The whole world will sink into a serious economic depression. Those in the so-called advanced and developed world will be hardest hit, while those who have been writhing in poverty during these years of inflation and plenty will see little difference in their sort, for how could they get poorer? The giant economic bubble that inflated over the past fifty years and exacerbated the inequities between north and south, developed and underdeveloped will pop.

Finally, the cycle will end. Ever remembering that in every war during this period, the warring parties are on the same side and are manipulated to make war so that The Dark Forces may reap more gain, but the light of the Brotherhood shines ever intensely on the situation, directed there by the good souls on earth. Like two adolescent boys who begin by "horsing around" and eventually end up fighting, the warring parties will be caught up in their own insanity and destroy themselves. The markets will repeat their final plunge and the world's economy will stand silent. The benighted ones will have accumulated much of the world's wealth on their side, only to find that wealth worthless as the currencies collapse.

### State of Dispossession to Change Mankind

If the mass of humanity allows the process of dispossession to take place without protest, and this seems to be the present state of mass compliance, then perhaps once they have nothing left, they may be ready to listen to the God-Within. No force can take away the soul, although some have tried. No force can steal one's intelligence, will to live, knowledge and spirit. Dispossessed of all the material accoutrements, will mankind rediscover the smell of the rose, the dew drops on the leaves, the sea breeze floating in from the vast ocean.

Community, self-help, mutual cooperation, creativity, a true sense of money, and its uses, barter, and most of all, the substance of soul that the God-Within can provide will keep the true souls of earth going as the towers of The Dark Forces crumble about them.

People will stop to listen to the new teachings of the Brotherhood that will come from the World Teacher and the seeds of the New Age will be truly planted. As communities band together to survive, the last remnants of The Dark Forces will have to be expurgated from earth but not without a last struggle.

## Threatened Bureaucracies Resort to War

With no jobs, no businesses, no savings, and moreover no tax base to exploit, tax revenues will shrink considerably. Bureaucracies will lose their sole source of sustenance. Those on the lower ranks of the bureaucracies, who thought they had a secure job for life, will lose their jobs. Those on the top tier will fight to survive, to preserve the huge cash cow that has served them so well. Many ministries and government services will be curtailed for lack of tax revenue.

The world is witness to numerous examples today where bureaucracies in impoverished countries have literally withered away from lack of tax revenue. Tax collectors can no longer squeeze any more money from impoverished people for fear of insurrection to their own lives. Yet even in the paucity, the bureaucracy still maintains its right to issue permits and create red tape for those it purports to serve. With only sporadic salaries, bureaucrats resort to under-the-table payments for the issuance of the most mundane paperwork such as licenses or permits. Anything that ever gets done in the bureaucracy is then the result of private fees paid to key bureaucrats. Eventually, the population realizes that there is little semblance of enforcement of these regulations, and the empty ministries eventually pass into irrelevance.

As more and more doors close in the bureaucracies, it will become evident that those who survive the squeeze will be those who hijacked the government structures years before. The military, police and intelligence forces—again those martial specialties so characteristic of the benighted Atlantean souls—will take their last stand.

Since they lack any productive capacity of their own, they will turn to war to keep their bureaucracies alive. Arms factories will buzz and people will be put to work making war. The wars and conflict we see today are merely preparing the mass humanity for an even greater and more widespread warfare. Terrorism, an invention of these forces, keeps a nebulous international threat in the minds of the masses, and enables the real perpetrators of war to capitalize on this threat that can be trumped up at will.

The surviving governmental forces will try to make people accept that war is the only way to keep the economy alive, and indeed as warmongering activities are thrown into action, the economies of the winners will buzz. The prospects of jobs and an economic recovery will draw the helpless back into the hands of these forces. So shall the last stand of The Dark Forces be characterized by warfare, the very antipathy of creation.

This time, however, the Great Brotherhood of Light have launched Their own forces on earth. Never before in the history of this present civilization have there been so many reincarnations of the noblest and most heroic souls on earth ready to stand battle against these forces. Never before has the Brotherhood penetrated mankind with so much light and ideas, pouring forth counter ideas of love and peace through the force of the Feminine Ray of the Holy Mother energy.

And by dispossessing people of their material well being, The Dark Forces will encounter exactly the opposite of what they expect. They will meet head-on the people they have tried so many centuries to suppress, for this material dispossession will unleash the creative force of the universe, the God-Within each individual. As this force is awakened in each individual, the masses will finally come to the point where they will no longer be led like so many sheep by The Dark Forces. They will realize that they are gods and goddesses able to recognize the twisted voices that call on them to do their bidding, and they instead, will dig in and refuse to be moved. "No more wars. Enough!" they will scream as they storm the symbolic Bastille! And thus will come tumbling down the last vestiges of The Dark Forces' empire.

Anyone who comes to their defense will be struck down, for they will stand out as sore thumbs. No longer will they be able to hide, for not only will acceleration automatically bring them to the surface, but people will recognize them for what they are. And one-by-one will they be thrust off the planet never to return. The Great and Holy Master Sanctus Germanus and his disciples will be in place to lead the clean up.

## Some Practical Suggestions

### Dealing with Insanity

Insanity engulfs our planet, but when you are engulfed in a fog, you intuitively seek the light, for it's your only way out. Now you know what to expect.

What you have seen is only the beginning. Expect more insanity to come. It would be unrealistic to think that it won't. But know this—you will not get caught or lost in it, even though you might have temporarily slipped, just a little bit, as one might walk in through a large puddle of mud. Just because you have slipped does not mean you need be soaked in mud. Regain your balance as you can. Take a bit of leisure. Get away from whatever it is that is stressful, but more than anything, call to the Great Lords of the Brotherhood for help, for they stand waiting to issue help, for according to cosmic law, they can only help mankind if you invite them through prayer or invocation!

So, do not be overwhelmed by the insanity that is overtaking the planet. Recognize it and when it seems to want to play through you, know that as well. Be not ashamed of it, neither reprimand your loved ones when they exhibit it, but help each other get through it as best as you can.

Know that this Armageddon is like a sort of plague of a very physical nature that will cause people to have temporary dementia, to go crazy, whatever, to throw something at you. Know that it is temporary that it passes, and afterward you should be so happy to have your loved ones back, safe and sane, for then you should have passed through that photon belt, that which causes this insanity we are already beginning to pass through.

But always remember that while the insane are insane, always temporary of course, they may not know what they do and may strike out at you. So beware. Do not put yourself in that position, for it can create a rift and a resentment that might take a long time to heal. Take care.

If the vipers of insanity strike at you too many times, do not be a fool and think, "Oh, I can take it. I can stay around here for more." Such foolishness has been rewarded by a gravestone. So do not overestimate yourselves and do not underestimate insanity. And more than anything, do not underestimate the power of your inner True Self that which is intimately and consciously taking your next breath for you that which is a part of every molecule or cell of your physical body. It is not about to cast you away but is putting you through the nerve of insanity that you shall discover sanity (coming from the word *sane* or healthy) as the true natural state of things in the fourth dimension, which is where we shall be when the process is complete. The whole process should not take so long, perhaps a few more years. Then you will come out to a sane world. You will all be so happy, for those who insist on the insanity shall have gone with the insanity, swept off the planet.

**Money Matters**

As these towers of economic and financial control crumble, the world will experience a serious economic depression that will last several years. This situation will be temporary until the new form of economy that the Great Brotherhood of Light has planned can take root in the minds of men. However, the crumbling of the whole economic and financial superstructure will mean a bit of chaos in your daily lives. All assumptions about your life will be challenged, as those financial and governmental institutions that disappoint you reveal their true colors.

To be prepared for these challenging economic times, we would suggest you take the following precautions:

1. Get out of debt. This means paying off all consumer loans and credit card debts. If possible pay off the mortgage on your house.
2. Save as much cash (the Euro is preferable to the U.S. Dollar) as possible. Stash some of it in a secure place in your home.
3. Buy gold coins in case your paper cash suddenly becomes worthless.
4. Bank failures will become more prevalent, so deal only with banks that can offer a government guarantee of your savings or put some of the cash and gold in a safety deposit box or a secure safe in their house.
5. Stop unnecessary shopping even if your government and the media cheer you on to keep spending to help the economy. It is not your duty to save the economy by spending aimlessly and going into debt. Buy only that which is necessary and sell what you do not absolutely need for cash.
6. If you are still invested in stocks, real estate, or mutual funds, get out immediately and save what is left. These "investments" are not destined to come back for a very long time, if ever. What you salvage will be worth more in terms of buying power as deflation overcomes the economy

Moreover, just remember that the sorrow and suffering you will observe are temporary and portend something infinitely better in the form of a New Age.

**Personal Responsibility–The Key to Health**
Individuals do have the power to take personal responsibility for their own health to ensure they will not be at the mercy of mandatory medical intervention. There is a new undercurrent sweeping the world through the natural foods and alternative health movements, which allow people to essentially be in charge of their own health, for who knows more about your own body but yourself?

These virus outbreaks being purported by the media are in actuality, only the symptoms of the present human physical degeneration that has reached the biological level. Let us not forget that Cancer was the avenging killer of the Twentieth Century, now it is mutating viruses that attack on a deeper level the immune systems of humans. This has now become the new, fearful threat. Viruses are one of the oldest organisms on the earth. They have been in existence long before man arrived on the scene and mankind has lived with them at its inception. The fact that viruses, one of the simplest organisms on the planet, can attack and compromise the immune systems of the most evolved organism on the planet clearly demonstrates that the current way of eating and medical intervention has gone awry.

Also, there is a strong negative effect to taking the "magic pill," prescription medications and invasive medical procedures. We are not saying that individuals should not seek medical attention when it is warranted, but preventive, alternative health treatments can protect the godly human system from outside microbes and viruses. Preventive health treatment is key to living in balance through the accelerated cycle we are now living through as time speeds up. The Brotherhood has given humanity the fundamentals for living through these challenging times. Some of these are very ancient methods indeed, in the form of natural whole foods, homeopathy, aromatherapy, medicinal herbs, acupuncture, therapeutic message, energy medicine, etc.

As the economic system and world affairs in general have spiraled down into insanity, the human constitution has followed likewise. If people were not sick and unbalanced, how could they go insane? The forces of Light have provided all that is necessary for humanity to weather the Armageddon.

**Meditation**

Finally, as insanity engulfs our planet and people awaken to and sense it, they will seek their sanity, which is only found in their divinity. Some of you are not comfortable with that word Divinity because you probably have not visited your celestial parent, your Higher Self, recently. We suggest you do so, in your hearts and thoughts through regular meditation.

So the Armageddon is that terrible filter you must all pass through, and it might just get snagged on your own garments here and there. But you will not get combed out, for you are not knots or tangles but instead the oil in the hair of your Divine Mother. Slide on through! You will glide through this ocean of insanity. THIS IS THE LAST GREAT HURDLE OF THIS PLANET BEFORE IT REACHES ITS PATH TO ENLIGHTENMENT.

## The Year 2012

The Mayan calendar ends in the year 2012, a time that is embedded in the mass consciousness of mankind. Thereabouts, when everything, and we mean everything, reaches critical mass, the world will be transformed as never before. The Brotherhood has described this momentous event as the big POP, for it will be precisely that sound that will awaken everyone to his true nature. And they will look back and see all the turmoil, trials, and tribulations during their lifetime as part of a bad dream! This is the promise.

But do we have to wait until 2012? No, is the simple answer. Collectively, mankind can bring this marvelous day forward as soon as we want. 2008? 2010? For as more and more individuals wake up to the events around them, and see the truth that all the present turmoil is essentially a battle between light and darkness, they will be lifted from the fray and taken out of harm's way. Moreover, each individual prayer or invocation enlisting help from the Brotherhood is sent forth as one coming from a God or Goddess, for each individual is of God.

We cannot stop the above steamroller of events from taking place, for only through this filtering process can each individual's true colors be exposed and seen for what it is. Instead, each prayer, each invocation quickens the whole filtering process so that this bloody mess can be mopped up sooner and Peace, the threshold to the New Age, can come about much faster.

So it is in mankind's hands. We can bring about an end to this Armageddon in a matter of a few years or we can suffer through it. Whatever the time frame, the LIGHT forces will triumph, for they are already celebrating their victory on the higher planes!

# CHAPTER 8
## Period of Reconstruction

After the great changeover of 2012, there will ensue a period of reconstruction that will prepare earth for its full entry into the Age of Aquarius. According to some astrologers, this great event is estimated at between 2060 and 2100. Those who had predicted an earlier entry into the Aquarian Age can see by the events facing us today that we are still in transition.

When we speak of reconstruction, we do not mean rebuilding that which has been destroyed, for it is evident that what had been destroyed did not serve mankind. The reconstruction will take place primarily in the mind, based on entirely different footing, on cosmic laws.

The awakening to a life that is free of the influences of The Dark Forces will lift a tremendous burden off each individual. The sky will look bluer than you could ever imagine and the flowers will glow with such lovely titillating color and perfume that you will no longer be able to ignore them. You will be thankful for every breath of air you take in and you will feel truly happy for the first time. You will express a HUGE sigh of relief that the bad dream is over. Everything will look brighter and better. You will know it when it happens, for the situation will be so markedly different from what you currently perceived.

People will continue doing what they have been doing--going to work, to school, doing chores, visiting friends—but with an entirely new uplifted perspective, of real optimism and hope that they are on the brink of building a truly wonderful new world.

Despite the dire economic conditions, many will find sheer joy in the simple. They will barter or share things to fulfill their needs. Relationships if still intact will be enhanced, and the future will never seem rosier. Many will continue to work at their jobs, but will find new meaning there. They will create new opportunities with their fellow workers that are not based solely on salary or monetary gain but on how much good their common actions will do for their fellow man. Compatible family and friends will surround us all.

The lifting of negativity will clear the air for the host of spiritual guides and elementals that hover round earth to participate with those increasing number of clairvoyant and clairaudient incarnates on the earth plane. Those souls working against the interests of mankind on the astral plane will also be banished and will no longer be able to influence people telepathically.

Evolved beings on the higher planes, the Masters of Wisdom, will use telepathic means to guide their initiates and disciples on earth in the task of reconstruction. They will prepare the world to receive the teachings of the coming World Teacher on the media waves and the Internet, principles upon which mankind will implement reconstruction.

## Law of Hierarchy

In the absence of the old Atlantean institutions of domination, the cosmic Law of Hierarchy will kick in and fill the void. That the universe is and has always been organized in a hierarchy in order to preserve the wisdom that must be passed down from beings of superior intelligence to the masses of humanity will become evident. New forms of governance in line with the Law of Hierarchy will emerge as the Spiritual Hierarchy extends downward to the earth plane. The preservation of this structure ensures the quality and the pureness of the teachings.

## Re-Education of Mankind: The World Teacher

The Great and Holy Master Sanctus Germanus once said, "If they knew better, they would do better." This statement rings with the hope that mankind, given the proper education in the immutable cosmic principles and laws and their application to life on earth, can rebuild a world fit for the Aquarian Age. Indeed, the principle of freewill shall apply and mankind will be given yet another chance to learn the building blocks of wisdom to construct the New Age.

These teachings will emanate from the department of the Christ or World Teacher and will have been disseminated telepathically to receptive disciples preceding the period of reconstruction. A core of incarnate disciples and workers is already in place and will have been trained to reinforce the teachings of the World Teacher as it pours forth telepathically as well as through the mass communications networks to reeducate earth's population.

Communications will be vital in the remaking of the earth's institutions. During the dot.com craze of the

1990s, a massive fiber-optics communications infrastructure was laid upon the seabed joining all continents. This network is the brainchild of the Great and Holy Master Sanctus Germanus, and remains at the bottom of the sea protected from the turmoil of the Armageddon. At the appropriate time prior to the awakening, this network will be reactivated and a new surge in broadband Internet technology will ensue that will make today's advances seem quite primitive. Every television set and computer will be able to connect to this high-speed communications network. This Super-Internet technology will play an incalculable unifying role in the years of reconstruction to come.

In addition, throughout the Armageddon period, the wireless satellite telecommunications systems will remain intact. These marvelous systems of communication will bring about a truly advanced form of the Internet that will link all corners of the globe in a way never before known. It is the precursor of the principle of oneness. Even now, access to the world via the Internet is possible, but the future will bring even greater possibilities, so that individuals and groups of individuals will interact with great ease with similar counterparts all around the world. No longer will information be the monopoly of the big broadcasting systems.

An individual will be able to produce a movie and disseminate it in a far more efficient way than the present mode of distribution. Think of the wireless communications and how people today carry upon their person the makings of full computers and instant communications upon the airwaves. There will be no need for cumbersome wires. You will be able to carry your computer anywhere in the world and still remain connected to the Internet. These forms of instant communication are the precursors of telepathic communications that will follow.

The highly sophisticated fiber optics network and wireless telecommunications systems await the coming of the World Teacher, for this time He comes not necessarily in the form of a man, like Jesus or Buddha, but more as a set of cosmic governing principles that will be disseminated in all forms of media presentation--films, talk programs, educational classes, games, and the like--into the far corners of the earth on this broadband communications network. The extent to which humanity absorbs these principles will determine the extent to which human society can carry on in self-governing units, quite unlike the preponderant governmental structures of the Piscean era.

Those in charge of the dissemination of these principles are now being trained for this task. That you must readily conjure up visions of Big Brother bearing down on and brainwashing the human populations would be natural given our experience during the Twentieth Century. However, when you imagine a world minus the negativity of The Dark Forces, there will be no oppression or domination involved in the use of these systems for the enlightenment of mankind.

The principles of the World Teacher emitted through the Internet will be that which govern the universe. They are powerful principles backed by the Love and Will of God. And so far, over the past millions of years, the universe has been doing quite well and in good hands! "By their fruits, ye shall judge them." The teachings of the World Teacher shall be judged on the basis of how it affords the individual soul its path toward liberation.

Earth must fall into line with the other planets

under this holy governance, for that which causes every atom to orbit in its own sphere in total harmony with the rest of creation must prevail on earth.

## Remaining Human Resistance

At the point of the great awakening, we can only hope that mankind will use this insight to rebuild the earth in line with higher principles. Their understanding at that point of the higher principles will be no higher than at the point before the great pop. The main difference will be the absence of The Dark Forces that made life so difficult in all endeavors.

This does not imply that everyone at the time of the reconstruction will be in agreement with one another. Just as the hierarchal structure is based on the individual's spiritual development, differences in intelligence, and levels of understanding among individuals will exist. The differences, however, will not be translated into domination of one over the other. Discussions over policy or community decisions will take on a different flavor, one of constructive building, each voice adding constructively to the formulation of policy rather than the backstabbing, political posturing, and outright sabotage that often characterize today's political process.

In this new atmosphere, man must still face the weaknesses and strengths within himself. No longer will he be able to lay the blame on others or on negative circumstances. The new conditions put forth before him will favor his spiritual growth, IF he chooses to go that path. The principle of freewill will remain intact, but the choices will be subtler. There will no longer be the hard-hitting manipulations and twisted logic for good and bad emanating from negative forces to confuse mankind. The only confusion that will remain is within man himself, and if he listens to his soul, the path out of this confusion will be lit.

So then, one of the main tasks in the initial stages of the reconstruction is to reeducate mankind to look inward, into his soul and to explore the **inner space,** which is in essence the reality of all things.

## Remaking Human Society: The Return to Earth's Bosom

We mentioned in the previous chapter the acceleration the earth is going through to catch up with its evolutionary schedule. We as inhabitants on earth are carried along this wave of acceleration and are in a sense forced to either evolve with earth or get off. Those who remain on earth after the Armageddon will have elected to stay, moving with earth into greater light. There will be many who will elect not to stay and pass on to other evolutions in the universe.

Since the great LOGOS, the spirit that inhabits the body of earth, will have evolved further along its path, those who remain on earth will find many of the answers to their individual evolutionary search in the earth. There will be a de-emphasis of the urban area and a return to the land. People, as one of the Brothers puts it, will scratch the earth with their feet to find the wisdom that was there in the past. During the great economic depression of the Armageddon, food shortages will have driven people out of the cities to seek more stable supplies of food in the countryside. More people will take up farming and gardening to supplement their tables, and their children will reengage in the hard but satisfying work of cultivating food. This trend will bring people back into contact with the earth and closer to their salvation. The towers of the city do not hold the answer to the liberation of man's soul.

Part of what earth will bring to our understanding is that ALL so-called ethnic religions are valid, for the Great Brotherhood of Light placed gods and goddesses on different parts of the earth for a specific purpose—to communicate to those living in those localities the ancient wisdom at the level that they could understand. Yet for centuries, other more aggressive religions, primarily Christianity and Islam, hijacked by The Dark Forces, systematically destroyed these earth gods and goddesses and imposed their brand of belief on others. ALL ethnic religions and beliefs will be renewed and will allow mankind to rekindle its contact with the earth. After a period of time, they will realize that these ethnic beliefs are indeed all coming from the same source, the Almighty God.

In the spiritual dimension, there is currently a committee of former religious leaders working diligently to harmonize the scriptures of earth's fractious religions so that eventually ALL religions and beliefs will come under ONE world religion, taught by the World Teacher. The closer to earth mankind looks, the closer it will come to the realization that there is only ONE religion.

## Cities No Longer Dominant

Many of the large cities that flourished as financial centers of the world will be considerably diminished in size and influence. Some backwater areas such as Canada and South America will rise as centers of learning, culture and the arts and will lead the world in its course to reconstruction. People will no longer be forced to flock to the cities for opportunities because what they are looking for will be available in their homes via more advanced forms of the Internet. In other words, they will not be obliged to live in urban areas to survive, and the free

## Period of Reconstruction

choice of where one wants to live will be available to all.

Communities will band together to rebuild their different localities. The destruction of the Armageddon will have been very selective and aimed at that which did not serve mankind. All that is useful will survive. Much of the preponderant government presence will no longer exist as it withers away for lack of tax revenue and relevance. People will thus set up self-governing bodies at the local level, and to their great surprise, will find they can get along without the top heavy government structure above them. They will realize that their governments were really doing very little to help them, except to overtax and drain their resources with their non-productive activities. Freedom from the yoke of governments and their insatiable needs will be one of the hallmarks of the Period of Reconstruction.

Who should keep law and order then? In the Period of Reconstruction, the earth will be rid of those elements that caused so much contention and conflict that huge police and defense structures came to dominate government spending. With these elements eliminated, the police and military will be relics of the past and people will be guided by principle instead. The one-man sheriff concept will return.

Communities will recognize the need to maintain essential transport, communications, and educative infrastructure in their respective locales and will coordinate with one another to interconnect with each other. As for the surviving national infrastructures such as the super highways and air and sea transport lanes, communities will have to decide if these are indeed necessary for the ultimate achievement of soul liberation. How much consumerism will exist will ultimately depend on mankind's orientation, a choice he will be given once again. Will there be a need to transport thousands of containers of goods as we do now or will we fulfill our God-given abilities to think things into existence? Will we again displace ourselves to rely on great transport machines such as trains, airplanes, or ships, or will we develop our innate abilities to appear in places we wish to be instantly–through astral travel? These are the awesome choices before mankind in the New Age.

## Basis of Group Structure

During the past centuries, communication with the so-called dead on the vast astral plane gives us an idea of how life on earth may be organized. Testimonies from those who have left the body but still reside in a more refined physical (etheric) body, unseen to the physical five senses, reveal life without the toil of survival, "making a living" earning enough money to pay the rent and feed the kids—life where one need only think of a Tudor house to live in and it is thus or of having afternoon tea and it is thus, etc.

Mankind as a whole may not reach this level of development but such an advance in spiritual evolution is achievable. The reeducation of mankind will reorient man's outlook and goals toward the innate abilities generated from the God-Within. They will pattern themselves against new heroes instead of the Marlboro cigarette man, rock singers, or tycoons. The Masters of Wisdom of the Great Brotherhood of Light will serve as examples of what individual souls can achieve while yet on the earth plane.

All institutions NOT serving the interest of mankind will be destroyed in the period of the Armageddon. In line with the basic cosmic Law of Attraction, those of similar vibrations will band together to form groups as wide and divergent as you can imagine, yet all having their source in the one Godhead. Individuals will almost instantly be put in contact with those whom they are most compatible in the most natural way. The great complex of ideas that make up God's creation is yet beyond limited human reasoning, but the groups that will make up the human society shall reflect the multiple diversity of the Mind of God and bring out all the richness of the Creation.

Since it is the vibratory level of the souls that draw together individuals, there will be no conflict within the groups. Not only will the vibratory levels of each group be in harmony, their specific purpose according to the divine plan will also be in synchronization with their vibratory levels. Everyone and every group will be imbued with divine purpose as the new teachings of the World Teacher flood the mass consciousness of mankind. Those who resist these trends will simply have to change planets.

## Transitional Changes

The vestiges of the world today will be gradually phased out over time. There will come a time when money, banks, and economy will no longer exist as we know it today. As soul liberation advances, mankind will gain the skills to mentally meet his needs. He will be able to invoke Divine Will to meet his needs, much like the etheric dimension that hovers above the physical. If the individual soul desires a certain house, he may "will it" into being. If another prefers to live under the stars, that is his choice. The ultimate freedom comes when the individual soul can truly do what it desires without harming his neighbor.

Such a free organization can only exist on higher

material planes, such as the etheric plane. Mankind will rediscover this etheric vision and the ability to prosper on that plane, while the vestiges of the dense physical world institutions will have to serve his needs. However, without the conflict and barriers inherent in the presence of The Dark Forces, mankind will witness a speed and accuracy of evolution like never before.

## Resolution of Hunger

As part of earth's evolution into a higher cycle, weather conditions during the Period of Reconstruction will favor bumper crops. Food will grow abundantly throughout the earth's surface so that no one group will control food production and use it to broker influence. Evenly dispersed agricultural production will provide all local communities with food, so that one area is not dependent upon the other for survival. The goal of food self-sufficiency, so desired by all, will be achieved.

The hungry belly shall be no more, for hunger was but a means of control, a means of keeping parts of the world oppressed, so that wealth could be concentrated in certain areas for fuller exploitation. As the reconstruction advances, changes in the geological make-up of the earth will open up viable crop lands in South America, Canada and present desert areas. Great stretches of fertile virgin land, which by design have been held in trust during these years of turmoil, will come available for food and industrial crop cultivation.

Can you imagine agriculture without need for pesticides and fertilizers? That is what lie under the ice caps, in the deserts, and in the jungles of today. These regions will play a prominent role during the Period of Reconstruction.

## The Banking System

The banking system during the Period of Reconstruction will undergo a rapid decline as these towers of inequity collapse, however their distribution infrastructure, such as the electronic movement of money, will be preserved for a period of time. Spiritual adepts trained in banking will manage the banking system during this transition period.

At the end of the Armageddon and during the beginning of the Period of Reconstruction, people will have set up a system of bartering in the absence of any money of value. Money energy, stored in various places on the earth, primarily in the form of gold, will be distributed through the bank infrastructure. For a short transition period, some vestiges of paper money can be exchanged for gold units. All will get their equal share in order to purchase what they need outside their normal bartering to meet daily needs.

A new system of currency will be one of the first orders of business in the Period of Reconstruction. The general economic deflation that would have taken place during the Armageddon period should return the value of goods and services to their lowest common denominator. When this point is reached, gold as the standard of currency will again come into effect and fix the values on a solid basis.

The free exchange of goods and services can only really come about if there is a common world currency based on a common value, such as gold.

## Relevance of the Arts

The arts, music, and sciences will flourish, and the twisted forms will be released. Look at the order of nature. That is the pattern for the future arts and sciences.

Forms and sounds will rise up as the earth evolves spiritually. A new openness to energies from other planets will fuel a certain cosmic richness in the arts and sciences, and as a result, the arts will cool and tranquilize the psyche of man, enabling him to progress up the ladder of evolution in the most intelligent manner. The sciences will open up new vistas and breakthroughs that render physical life easier.

## Geological Changes

More geological changes will take place during this century of great change. All efforts to preserve the status quo of the atmosphere will be for naught because with the current acceleration of the earth's evolution, more energy than ever is being poured down onto the earth plane. This is the energy that makes some people go insane but as it relates to the atmosphere and geography of the earth, it will have profound effects. The two ice caps on the south and north poles will very rapidly melt down causing the oval shape of the earth to change to a spherical one. This will cause a natural shift in the axis that will have ramifications on the present geography of the world. Many low lying areas will be flooded, and old seas that existed, for instance, in the Sahara, the Gobi, and the Death Valley deserts will fill up again. This will have a profound effect on the surrounding climate and open up much rich arable land for future agriculture. These changes will occur gradually over the course of this century and should be completed by the time we enter the Aquarian Age.

As part of the geological changes on earth, certain land masses may rise up out of the sea that were once part of the ancient civilizations of Lemuria and Atlantis. These lands will lay bare for many decades, until the land has been leeched of the unwanted sea salts, and can be opened for agricultural development. Buried also in these subcontinents are an unknown wealth of minerals and elements that will be necessary for the technological advances that will come about in the New Age.

After a period of leeching, these subcontinents will contribute greatly to the supply of oxygen in the earth's atmosphere as dense forests and vegetation already seeded grow into place.

## Making of a New World Union

The reconstruction of a new world union would be the natural outcome of the battle between light and darkness. The victor, the forces of light, would naturally align a new world order with the Spiritual Hierarchy, for only in that way could mankind's evolution reflect the more spiritual track the earth will have taken. To set the world aright will require a group comprising adepts and initiates who have so long toiled in the back rooms of power to influence world leaders. They will telepathically guide mankind in building a new world order.

We mentioned that in the initial years of the Period of Reconstruction the reeducation of mankind in cosmic laws and principles will take precedence over all activities. The hierarchy that stretches forth from the Office of the World Teacher to the man on the street will pour forth teachings to uplift humanity with a knowledge of cosmic principles and laws. Spiritual guides will coach individuals telepathically, media programs will lay forth examples of the principles, adepts and their disciples will come forth to teach in new mystery schools, and universities, and the school systems will finally grasp the underlying basis of all that they teach.

Once these principles and cosmic laws have been

grasped and understood by the leaders, mankind will be left to its own devices to rebuild a new world order. Some indications are given below:

### The Passing of the Nation-State

The role of nation-states in the lives of mankind will gradually fade out, as its true colors as an instrument of war and conflict come to light. A relatively recent invention, the world we see today divided into a couple hundred nation-states grew out of past monarchal kingdoms, then imperial empires, and finally, the post-World War II decolonization. As a secular state, it represented at one time a step in the liberation of mankind from the dark concepts of church, but unfortunately, it took other forms of oppression.

The concept of nation-state sovereignty within clearly defined territorial borders promotes a state-level selfishness that allows its leaders to oppress their citizens with a range of bestial techniques, including physical torture, and mass horrors. State sovereignty also allows leaders to control and manipulate the thinking of the people within their borders, feeding them when they are good, and starving them when they are naughty. The whole range of horrors to oppress mankind takes place under the guise of state sovereignty. So, the concept of the nation-state once thought to free mankind from the shackles of religious oppression was merely hijacked by The Dark Forces to promote the "kingly syndrome."

In line with the Atlantean characteristics of the Dark Forces, the nation-state became the unit of warfare, having led the world more times than desired into war and destruction of worldwide proportions. Today, it is on the level of the state that the great military forces are built and deployed, and with this military power, one nation-state can oppress another or force others to make war. Even civil wars grow out of the desire to create two separate nations out of one. Thus, the nation-state has served The Dark Forces well, for it provided them with the vehicle to accomplish their two specialties of money accumulation (through forced taxation) and warmongering. Part of the awakening will be the realization that the nation-state will no longer be useful. This implies that the state, province, district, and urban administrative units may also be considered outmoded. New organizations will rise out of their ashes during the Period of Reconstruction that will reflect the New Age groupings linked through advanced broadband and telecommunications networks, outside the limitations of the nation-state. Today, we see how the Internet has overridden many areas of the traditional nation-state jurisdiction. More of these breakdowns will become apparent in the coming years. More we cannot say at this present time, for much depends on how mankind will collectively create alternative units.

## Benevolent Hierarchy

If aligned to cosmic principles and laws, the new world order would necessarily be an extension of the Spiritual Hierarchy of the Great Brotherhood of Light, for the march upward in individual spiritual evolution must necessarily follow the path blazed by the Sisters and Brothers, the Masters of the Brotherhood. Whatever level we find ourselves on in the new world hierarchy of the Period of Reconstruction and eventually the Aquarian Age, the path of ultimate soul liberation has already been mapped out for us.

Bits and pieces of the divine plan for earth are revealed with each passing day. Today, we know that its main goal, promoted by its major exponent, the Great and

Holy Master Sanctus Germanus, is that of Soul Liberation. All actions of mankind must be done with that lofty goal in mind.

# Postscript

All things are truly for the sake of good. To dispel the myth of the Armageddon as something to be dreaded and avoided is to understand the great Good that the Creator always bestows upon His children. How could we possibly usher in a Golden Age without first purging the earth of all that is ignorant and dark? So let us go forth with courage and steadfastness, bearing the turmoil of the coming years and knowing that the Armageddon will ultimately make our world more perfect.

A sequel to this book will follow and will provide further guidance for the latter part of the Armageddon. It will also prepare thought for the coming Period of Reconstruction, which is of crucial importance, for the choices mankind makes then will determine his course into the Age of Aquarius.

ISBN 141200373-3